FOLLOWING THE WAY

OTHER TITLES BY GERALD O'COLLINS, S.J.,
AVAILABLE FROM PAULIST PRESS

Luke and Acts (1993)
Retrieving Fundamental Theology (1993)
The Bible for Theology (1997)
All Things New (1998)
The Tripersonal God (1999)
A Concise Dictionary of Theology:
   Revised and Expanded Edition (2000)

RELATED TITLE AVAILABLE FROM PAULIST PRESS

The Convergence of Theology: A Festschrift Honoring
   Gerald O'Collins, S.J. (2001)

FOLLOWING THE WAY
JESUS, OUR SPIRITUAL DIRECTOR

GERALD O'COLLINS

Paulist Press
New York/Mahwah, New Jersey

Cover design by Ray Lundgren

First published in Great Britain by Fount,
an imprint of HarperCollins Publishers,
under the title: FOLLOWING THE WAY.

ISBN: 0-8091-3984-7

Published in the United States by
Paulist Press
997 Macarthur Boulevard
Mahwah, New Jersey 07430

www.paulistpress.com

Printed and bound in the
United States of America

CONTENTS

DEDICATION

To the memory of Raymond Brown (1928–98),
a very great scholar and dear friend.
I regret that it is only after his passing to the Lord
that I have come up with this study of the parables.
I hope Ray approves.

INTRODUCTION

Our spiritual needs are less easily satisfied than our physical needs. We want to be enlightened and guided in our journey to God. Who can provide us with the light and strength we need and desire? All power to spiritual directors, soul friends and gurus of every kind! Yet it is vital to realize that in Jesus we have 'the' spiritual director to end all spiritual directors. Of course, he wants us to seek help from our brothers and sisters, whom he has called to live with us and lead us in the community he founded. When we worship with them and profit from their teaching, they can show us the way to follow. At the same time, however, we dare not neglect the wealth of wisdom which the Gospels offer us from Jesus himself, who is the divine Wisdom come among us in person.

Jesus conveys enlightenment in many ways. In this book I plan to limit myself to his parables, those simple-sounding yet amazingly profound stories that show us how the final kingdom of God is already taking shape among us. Jesus proves himself to be our spiritual director by being 'the' story-teller of all time. Jesus does not tell these stories simply 'to point a moral and adorn a tale'. Much more than mere picturesque illustrations, his parables question us, challenge the normal standards and securities of our lives, call for our whole-hearted response, and invite us to walk in radically different ways. This final reign of

God comes as sheer gift from our God's incredible loving kindness, a gift that we must receive with ecstatic joy and appropriate with utter confidence. The personal power of God is setting things right in our world. We should acknowledge God's sovereign power and Jesus as the Lord of the kingdom already present in our midst.

Jesus' parables reveal a new world and a new way of living. But they do so through language and pictures that seem quite familiar and very ordinary, even if at times he gives his storyline unusual and even extraordinary twists. Jesus tells us of two brothers, one who runs away and one who stays at home. He introduces day-labourers who work in vineyards, and managers of large estates. He brings in women searching for lost property or preparing dough for the oven. His stories present a lazy judge, a merchant hunting for precious jewels, a traveller robbed and left for dead, servants waiting up at night for their master to return. These parables take us into the mind and heart of Jesus. They let us glimpse his vision of the world around him.

These stories answer our questions: What is God like? And how is God dealing with us in these last times? Jesus' parables hold out to us his vision of the incredible generosity of our heavenly Father. Through his stories Jesus wants to share his insights with us and gently coax us into opening ourselves to God's final rule over our lives. If this book helps more of you to catch these insights and receive the divine offer with joy, I will be deeply satisfied. If you have never read the parables, please begin now and discover their remarkable impact. They will work their spell on you when you read them and let them enter your life of prayer.

Gerald O'Collins, S.J.
Gregorian University, Rome

PART ONE

GOD'S INITIATIVE

CHAPTER ONE

THE PRODIGAL SON

Then Jesus said, 'There was a man who had two sons. The younger of them said to his father, "Father, give me a share of the property that belongs to me." So he divided his property between them. A few days later the younger son gathered all he had and travelled to a distant country, and there he squandered his property in dissolute living. When he had spent everything, a severe famine took place throughout that country, and he began to be in need. So he went and hired himself out to one of the citizens of that country, who sent him to his fields to feed the pigs. He would gladly have filled himself with the pods the pigs were eating; and no one gave him anything. But when he came to himself he said, "How many of my father's hired hands have bread enough and to spare, but here I am dying of hunger! I will get up and go to my father, and I will say to him, 'Father, I have sinned against heaven and before you; I am no longer worthy to be called your son; treat me like one of your hired hands.'" So he set off and went to his father. But while he was still far off, his father saw him and was filled with compassion; he ran and put his arms around him and kissed him. Then the son said to him, "Father, I have sinned against heaven and before you; I am no longer worthy to be called your son." But the father said to his servants, "Quickly, bring out a robe – the best one – and put it on him; put a ring on his finger and sandals on his feet. And get the fatted calf and kill it, and let us eat and celebrate; for this son of mine was dead and is alive again; he was lost and is found!" And they began to celebrate.'

(Luke 15:11–24)

From childhood we have all been delighted by stories in which animals and birds are endowed with intelligence and the power of speech. We may even have learned something from films and fables in which cats, dogs, foxes, mice, pigs, rabbits, rats and even ducks have interesting things to say and do. Centuries before Christ, Egyptian and Greek story-tellers spread fables in which animals played comic roles and also communicated perennial wisdom. In the twentieth century, Kenneth Grahame's *Wind in the Willows* has charmed generations with its account of Toad, Mole, Ratty, Badger and other animals. The seven children's fantasies by C.S. Lewis which appeared from 1950 to 1956, *The Chronicles of Narnia*, used 'intelligent' animals to entertain, enlighten and edify his readers. The Old Testament includes at least one talking animal, Balaam's donkey (Numbers 22:28–30). The Christian Bible includes one eagle who cries out a message as it flies through mid-heaven (Revelation 8:13).

But Jesus gives no such talking roles to animals and birds. His stories feature human beings. Animals and birds enjoy only marginal roles, like a lost sheep the shepherd searches for, some pigs fed by the prodigal son, the fatted calf his father has killed for a feast, or the animal the good Samaritan uses for carrying the wounded traveller. Jesus talks of barnyard hens, sparrows and other birds of the air. But we never hear a word from these animals or birds, still less anything from trees that talk. Talking trees have a notable place in the Book of Judges (9:8–15). Much later, at the end of the seventh century or the beginning of the eighth century AD, an Anglo-Saxon poem, 'The Dream of the Rood', has the cross on which Christ died speak and recall its feelings during the crucifixion. But we hear nothing from trees in Jesus' parables, not even from the mustard tree he celebrates for offering generous shelter and protection.

Through his parables Jesus evokes a range of human experiences – things that happen to men and women frequently or at least every now and then. His stories reflect vividly how he sees our lives and cherishes the powerful and loving way God deals with us. They answer our questions: What is God like? What is God doing for us? The parables of Jesus share with us his new vision of our world and the fresh possibilities God offers us. Let us begin with the story of the prodigal or lost son. It opens with an experience of human loss and ends with an amazing sense of God's overwhelming love for us. The story could well be renamed 'the parable of the merciful father' — the longest and loveliest parable Jesus has left us.

THE SETTING IN LUKE

One of the commonest and most painful human experiences is the experience of loss. Through death and other causes, we lose our relatives and friends. We will lose opportunities. Sooner or later we must lose our strength and our health. We can lose our sense of direction, that clear recognition of where our task in life should be taking us. Day by day we suffer the loss of time, and we lose one thing on every occasion that we choose something else.

At a funeral I recently attended, a middle-aged woman uplifted everyone with her rich and full voice when she led us in hymn-singing and then sang some antiphons solo. Years ago Dolores had been auditioned in New York and invited to sing musicals for Rogers and Hammerstein. But she decided to marry and raise a family at home in Philadelphia. Recalling her still spectacular voice, I wondered whether footfalls echo painfully in her memory. Could she and should she have done otherwise?

Luke gathers together in chapter 15 three stories that Jesus tells us about some loss, followed by a finding and great joy: the parables of the lost sheep, the lost coin and the lost son. The first two (shorter) parables deal with people who have searched for something they have lost. A shepherd leaves his flock and hunts for one sheep which has strayed away from the other ninety-nine sheep; a woman ransacks her dimly lit cottage until she finds the one coin that has fallen out of the purse in which she keeps her ten silver pieces.

Those two stories are not concerned with the fact that the woman, even after losing her coin, still has ninety per cent of her wealth, and the shepherd still has ninety-nine per cent of his flock. The stories aim rather at evoking a sense of the loss itself – the irritation and pain which the disappearance of even a little money or livestock can cause.

Of course, the losses are slight: ten per cent of the woman's cash and only one per cent of the shepherd's flock.[1] Yet such small losses can prove painful and frustrating. The recovery can be even more joyful, encouraging and heartening than making the ten silver pieces or raising the hundred sheep was in the first place.

Jesus tells these stories to evoke that common feeling. He does this to open up a vision of God's astoundingly merciful love towards sinful men and women. God is utterly glad to find and welcome back those who have gone astray and been lost. Along with everyone in heaven, God is full of joy over even one sinful person who repents.

In the two parables of the straying sheep and the missing coin, Jesus talks of lost property and does so from the point of view of the human loser, not from that of the lost. He has nothing to say, for instance, about the experience of the sheep that went astray. How does it feel when night is falling and it cannot find its way back to the flock? Has it become terrified when it hears the barking of dogs and the howling of wild animals? (The two stories, admittedly, both make a brief reference to repentance, but leave it unexplained. In any case, it makes little sense to attribute repentance to the lost sheep, still less to the lost coin.) The parable of the prodigal son tells, however, of the boy's experiences when lost and of his repentance when found.

THE RETURN TO GOD

This is a story of a farmer's younger son who is anxious about his freedom. He wants independence, the chance to break with tradition, to get away from a family life that smothers him, and to set up elsewhere on his own.[2] Life at home has become a burden to him. He secures his share of the inheritance from his father, converts it into hard cash, waves goodbye and heads for a distant country and freedom. Predatory 'friends' and high living eat up the money. The boy runs through his inheritance and is caught penniless when an economic crisis hits the country.

Instead of doing what a practising Jew should do – namely, look for the nearest Jewish community where he could find help and work – the prodigal son attaches himself to a Gentile farmer. He is sent out into the fields to work as a swineherd. For a good Jew there could hardly be any greater humiliation. Pigs are unclean. To act as a swineherd means incessant contact with these impure animals. The boy has effectively denied his religion. The sinner who began with prostitutes ends by becoming a thoroughly godless apostate.

For his work he receives far too little food. He would love to eat some of the pods being fed to the swine. But he counts for less than the animals, and is not allowed to get down with the pigs and share the food himself. In his hunger and humiliation he 'comes to himself' – a wonderful, poignant expression. He decides to go back to his father and to God. He remembers what he has lost. He will return home and say to his father: 'Father, I have sinned against heaven and in your eyes.' He has only low expectations of what will follow his confession. At best he hopes to be taken back on the property as a hired hand. He remembers the generous and kindly way his father treats even the hired hands; they have 'bread enough and to spare'. He pulls his shattered life together, and clings to the thought of his father like a life-raft.

As the boy approaches home, the father sees him coming, forgets his dignity and runs out to greet him. Up to that point in the story the father has said nothing – not a single word.[3] Now he begins to speak. He cuts short his son's apologies. He is not anxious to discuss matters – let alone impose conditions under which he might be willing to receive his son back into the household. The father does not even make some declaration of pardon.

Forgiveness is expressed by what the father does. The boy receives the robe given to an honoured guest. He is handed a ring to wear – presumably as a sign of his right to act again as a son. He is no longer allowed to go barefoot like a common labourer, but wears the sandals that the free son of a free farmer should wear. The lost son who has come home is taken into the house for a feast of joy.

There is much in this parable of the lost son which speaks to our condition today. It says something about that intriguing and fateful matter of decision-making. Our own lives, the lives of other people, and literature that we read constantly confront us with the mysterious process by which men and women make major decisions. Why, in T.S. Eliot's terms, did we decide not to take that passage, never to open that door, and not to go out into the rose garden? At the climax of Iris Murdoch's novel *The Sandcastle*, why does the hero choose to remain seated at the dinner-table, instead of rushing out after the girl with whom he has fallen in love? What happens when people face this kind of decision that can make or remake their lives either for good or for evil?

The prodigal son, we are told, 'comes to himself'. He is there in a distant country, caught in a situation of hunger and humiliation. But before he can find a way out of his appalling situation, he must first 'come to himself'. He has run away from so much – including himself. If you like, he now emerges from his self-alienation. He finds himself. No one is there to tell him to make his decision or to urge him to adopt any particular course of action. All alone he decides. He must find himself, before he finds his way out of his misery and back to his family.[4]

Back in 1968, a year of questioning and turmoil for many people of my generation, I happened to preach my first sermon on the prodigal son story. It was delivered to a student audience at the University of Tübingen in southern Germany. Sensing the midlife journey on which I then found myself, a German friend commented on the sermon with grim humour: 'Gerry, are you finding yourself among the foreign swine?' 'Yes,' I told him, 'I do feel a bit lonely, and I am trying to decide what I should do with myself.' But I felt that I couldn't leave it at that and assured him: 'You're certainly not swine; you are good friends of mine. In any case we are not suffering from a famine; and I feel very much at home in Germany. It's not a far country, as far as I am concerned.' Yet this friend had put his finger on my struggle to find myself, a struggle which I have always linked with the prodigal son's not rejecting himself and so being able to 'come to himself'.

THE FATHER'S LOVE

Beyond question, the parable shares with us a vision of sin and repentance and does so through the person of the younger son. But, by shifting the focus to his father, the story invites us to open ourselves to the amazing love of our compassionate God. Jesus does not use the noun or the verb 'love', but we will fail to appreciate the story he tells unless we think in terms of love. We can single out here at least four qualities of human and divine love.

Loved Back into Life

God's love is life-giving and creative; it brings into existence what has not yet existed. But even more remarkable is its 're-creative' force, which gives new life to what once existed and has died. The parable of the prodigal son presupposes the love with which his mother and father first gave him existence. The story highlights the overflowing love with which the compassionate father gives new life to his son who has died morally and religiously – a death which is far more serious and painful than a 'mere' physical death. 'This son of mine,' the father cries out, 'was dead and is alive again.' It is the father's love for his boy that makes this new life possible. He has loved him back into life.

Another father might well have become resigned to the disgraceful failure of his son. He could even have let himself become indifferent to the boy's fate, even quite apathetic about what would happen to him. But not the father of the prodigal son. Deeply concerned for the real interests of his son, he gives himself in love to the young scoundrel. His love expresses itself not merely through gifts like clothing, a ring and a family feast. It is the father's gift of himself to the returning prodigal that transforms the situation and makes all the difference.

I'll Be Loving You Always

This father knows only too painfully the situation to which his son has sunk, as one who is morally and religiously 'dead' and 'lost'. But he accepts him back with unconditional love, will never give him up, and cannot tolerate the idea of losing him forever. The French philosopher Gabriel Marcel (1889–1973) could have been commenting on Jesus' parable when he took the statement 'I love you' to mean: 'You must not die; you must live forever.' Those who love cannot tolerate the idea of the beloved no longer being there. Our loving God, revealed and reflected by the father of the prodigal son, delights in our being there. No matter how much we hurt and harm ourselves through sin, God's love is never withdrawn.

There is an edge of sadness to Gabriel Marcel's analysis of love, as there is to Irving Berlin's song 'I'll be loving you always'. When a friend first heard this lyric, he said to Berlin: 'Why don't you say, "I'll be loving you Thursday"? People can't love each other always.' This friend had a point. No matter how intensely and generously we love one another, how can we be sure that 'diamonds are forever'? Human relationships all too often lose their intensity and break down. In any case, our dear ones will be taken from us at the end. They will die, and cannot live with us forever. Irving Berlin was right, however, in refusing to change his words, 'I'll be loving you always'. They express our deep yearning to remain forever united with those whom we love.

Where merely human love runs up against the painful limits of its yearning, God's love will prevail. In this case, 'diamonds are forever'. The divine love offers something that human love alone can never achieve. It promises a new life, both here and hereafter. The joyful cry of the prodigal son's father, 'he is alive again', more than hints at what Jesus holds out to all of us: 'you are alive, and will never die. You will live at home with me forever.'

Giving and Receiving

Homecoming forms a further aspect of the divine love revealed through the story of the lost son. The loving father reaches out to welcome home his son who ran away. All true love reconciles and unites people. Of its very nature, love is a reciprocal force. It remains incomplete so long as its sentiments are not returned and there is not a full giving and receiving. Ultimately, love is like a hug; you cannot give one without receiving one yourself. For me to love someone necessarily means to hope that my feelings will be reciprocated. This is not a question of selfishly trying to manipulate or even force someone into loving me. It is a matter of the very nature of love itself as reciprocal.

In Jesus' parable the father's love is perfected when his sinful son who has been away 'in a distant country' comes home again. The father's love enables a new communion of life to open up and grow. The parable contains not the slightest hint of a distorted relationship in which the repentant son will now be smothered or even psychologically swallowed up by his father. Genuine love unites without being destructive. The greater the loving union, the more personal identity is safeguarded and enhanced. The father respected the wishes of the boy when he wanted to take his money and leave home. Now he welcomes him back with an exquisite respect that lets us glimpse the exquisite respect with which God waits for us and wants to enjoy a wonderful union of love with us. Like the father of the prodigal, God puts his arms around us, kisses us, and wants to be hugged in return.

A Feast of Joy

The homecoming of the young rascal leads at once to a family celebration. The fatted calf must be killed; love calls for a feast of joy. Jesus reminds us how joy, even indescribable joy, is woven into the very texture of love. Joy inevitably accompanies real love and all those occasions which in a particular way celebrate and express our love for one another: a birth, a baptism, a bar mitzvah, a wedding, an ordination, and even a funeral. We happily join our special friends or take part in family reunions. There is no more obvious spinoff from love than joy.

Year by passing year, young friends in Italy and elsewhere bless me by inviting me to 'do' their wedding. I always leave to them the choice of readings, prayers and hymns. But I find it delightful when they choose for the opening or closing hymn of the service Beethoven's 'Hymn to Joy', which begins 'Joyful, joyful, we adore Thee'. More than anyone else, the bride and bridegroom know how love begins and ends with ecstatic joy. By sharing with their families and friends their love, they share with them their special joy.

The boundless joy of God's compassionate love for us twice bursts through the parable of the prodigal son: to round off the first part of the story (Luke 15:24), and then again at the very end, when the father insists with his other son: 'We had to celebrate and rejoice, because this brother of yours was dead and has come to life; he was lost and has been found' (Luke 15:32). The last word about the divine love is that it will surprise us with joy – both in this life and in the life to come. Jesus has much to say about the boundless joy that our loving God holds out to us.

Over and over again in his preaching, Jesus brings in the image of a feast. He pictures our future life with God that way: 'Many will come from east and west and will eat with Abraham and Isaac and Jacob in the kingdom of heaven' (Matthew 8:11). But such joyful feasting does not have to wait till the end, when human history finishes. Right now Jesus happily eats with sinners and outcasts; he loves them and wants to bring them forgiveness and peace of heart. He is happy and at home with them. Luke's Gospel appreciates how joyful, forgiving love expressed by the parable of the prodigal son serves to defend Jesus' own practice when critics grumble and complain: 'This fellow welcomes sinners and eats with them' (Luke 15:2). Jesus' happiness is unbounded when prodigal sons and daughters come home and accept the divine love.

The last time I preached a sermon on the prodigal son, I was in the United States and helping in a downtown parish of Washington, D.C. After the service a middle-aged woman came to see me, her face radiant with joy. Tears of happiness glistened in her eyes when she said to me: 'Thank you, thank you, for that sermon. What you said has just happened to me. My brother who left our family and disappeared for more than twenty years has just come home again. It's utterly marvellous having him back.' I felt tears coming into my own eyes, and could do no more than grip the hand of the sister of the prodigal brother. Her brother had been lost and now was found. The one who had been dead was alive again. The ecstatic joy of that woman in Washington reflected the joyful love of our God who always welcomes home those who are lost and gone astray.

The Christian Bible ends with beautiful images of our heavenly homecoming when God promises to 'wipe every tear' from our eyes and take away all our 'mourning, crying and pain' (Revelation 21:4). In wonderfully imaginative ways the closing chapters of Revelation picture the destiny our loving God has prepared for us. It is no accident that the images which express the divine love include that of a marriage feast (Revelation

19:6–9). The joyful feasting that Jesus brings twice into his story of the prodigal son will find its fulfilment when the love of God blesses us with life that will never end.

WHAT IS GOD LIKE?

The parable of the prodigal son is the longest story Jesus has left us in answer to the question: What is God like? Without mentioning it, the first letter of John sums up very precisely what the parable is about: 'God is love' (1 John 4:8,16). Love is the most fundamental characteristic of our God.[5] In the late twentieth century scientists have searched for the holy grail of a 'grand unified theory' or 'GUT'. Jesus would encourage us to find out the grand unified theory in the divine love, the bond which reconciles, forgives and holds all people and all things together. One might boldly vary 1 John and say: 'God is our GUT, because God wants to hold all of us together in love.'

In his first encyclical letter, *Redemptor hominis* ('the Redeemer of human beings') of 1979, one that he sent around the world a year after becoming Pope, John Paul II wrote: 'Human beings cannot live without love. They remain incomprehensible to themselves, their life is senseless, if love is not revealed to them and if they fail to encounter love' (nr. 10). Through that letter and much else that he was going to say and do, the Pope wanted to assure all human beings that they don't have to live without love and plod their way through an apparently meaningless life. In his words and deeds and very presence among us, Jesus revealed that in God we encounter a boundless, undying love.

In the parable of the prodigal son Jesus tells a story that takes place over and over again when dissatisfied young men or women want to break with their families and indulge their freedom. But Jesus gives the story a most unusual twist: all too often when prodigals return home they may not find much love and hardly, if ever, the astonishingly merciful and unconditioned love with which the father of the prodigal son treats his sinful son. This story runs counter to what we might expect to happen when the young rascal trudges home.

The story also runs counter to what those who first heard this parable must have expected. They were used to the biblical stories of two or more brothers, in which the younger wins out over the older brother (or brothers). That was what happened in the Book of Genesis when the younger Jacob succeeded in getting the inheritance in place of Esau, and when Joseph triumphed over his older brothers. His father Jacob loved him 'more than any other of his children, because he was the son of his old age' (Genesis 37:3). Unlike the prodigal son, Joseph did not go willingly into a distant country, Egypt. He was sold in slavery. In that distant land he lost nothing but gained, as it were, everything when he became 'prime minister' to the pharaoh.

Jesus' story of the prodigal son offers a parody of such 'successful' younger brothers. Moreover, in this story the elder son is not beaten or excluded. Far from losing, he is invited, as we shall see, to take part in the family feast. Along with his brother he needs to be delivered from evil and enjoy a new family life. It is never said that the father loves the younger son more than the elder son. He loves both and cares for both in their different needs. All of this reflects Jesus' desire to establish a new brotherhood and sisterhood: 'Whoever does the will of God is my brother and sister and mother' (Mark 3:35).

Clearly we should let ourselves be astonished by Jesus' story rather than kill it with close analysis. I feel the impertinence of commenting on the love of God which comes through so powerfully. Hearing and being drawn into this story is infinitely preferable to indulging in abstract comments. Yet we may be helped to appreciate the parable a little more by remembering how the divine love is life-giving, eternal, welcoming and the trigger of lasting joy. These characteristics of God's love shine through the longest and most beautiful story Jesus ever told.

I suggest ending this chapter with two prayers and several exercises.

TWO PRAYERS

> O God, we praise and thank you for your endless love and mercy towards us.
> You bring us home to yourself and share with us your infinite happiness.
> You want us to be your sons and daughters, enjoying forever a loving communion of life with you.
> Fill us now and always with boundless joy at the greatness of your compassionate love towards each one of us.

> Father of mercy, like the prodigal son I return to you and say:
> 'I have sinned against you and am no longer worthy to be called your son.'
> Christ Jesus, Saviour of the world, I pray with the repentant thief to whom you promised Paradise:
> 'Lord, remember me in your kingdom.'
> Holy Spirit, fountain of love, I call on you with trust:
> 'Purify my heart, and help me to walk as a child of light.'

EXERCISES

1 Compose your own prayer in response to the parable of the prodigal son.
2 Imagine what the workers on the father's estate first said when the prodigal son left and then later when he came home.
3 What points does the parable have in common with the story of Zacchaeus (Luke 19:1–10)? Unlike the prodigal

son, Zacchaeus is identified by name, is presumably married, and does not leave home. Are there any further, deeper differences between that story and the parable of the prodigal son?

1 Here the stories of the lost sheep and the lost coin differ markedly from that of the prodigal son, in which someone loses a human being, who is one of his two sons.

2 Presumably the farmer's wife is still alive; they may have one or more daughters. We may presume that the elder son is married, and that a daughter-in-law and some grandchildren also live in the big home. Perhaps one or more parents of the farmer and his wife are still living. At all events, to account for 'let *us* eat and celebrate' (Luke 15:23) and '*we* had to celebrate' (Luke 15:32), one must think of other members of the household. But Jesus does not let us become distracted by the extended family. He tells a 'spare' story and concentrates on the dramatic interaction between three persons: the father and his two sons.

3 At the start of the parable when the younger son asks, 'Give me my share of the property', the father has nothing to say. He does not ask: 'Are you sure you want it all now?' Still less does he say: 'What's the problem? What's eating you up?'

4 As John Henry Newman and St Augustine of Hippo insist, we must come to ourselves and know ourselves if we are to come to and know God. This means accepting our sinful culpability and not banishing it to some impersonal realm by arguing: 'Mistakes were made.'

5 In 2 Corinthians 13:13, St Paul strikingly chooses love as *the* defining characteristic of the Father.

CHAPTER TWO

THE ELDER SON

Now the elder brother was in the field; and when he came and approached the house, he heard music and dancing. He called one of the servants and asked what was going on. He replied, 'Your brother has come, and your father has killed the fatted calf, because he has got back safe and sound.' Then he became angry and refused to go in. His father came out and began to plead with him. But he answered his father, 'Listen! For all these years I have been working like a slave for you, and I have never disobeyed your command; yet you have never given me even a young goat so that I might celebrate with my friends. But when this son of yours came back, who has devoured your property with prostitutes, you killed the fatted calf for him!' Then the father said to him, 'Child, you are always with me, and all that is mine is yours. But we had to celebrate and rejoice, because this brother of yours was dead and has come to life; he was lost and has been found.'

(Luke 15:25–32)

A TALE OF TWO SONS

This chapter brings us to the role played by the second son in Jesus' story of the merciful father. A fairly grim sort of person, he may be the elder of the two boys, but any advantage in age and family position does not stop him from behaving in a thoroughly adolescent fashion. He has been out working on what is obviously a large estate. Presumably he is coming home a little tired. When he hears the sound of music and dancing, one would expect him to brighten up and let himself feel, 'Hooray! What a nice surprise! It's great to come home to a party.' Instead of rushing inside to share in the celebration, he suspiciously questions a servant to find out what is going on.

The servant speaks well of the two persons at the heart of the party. 'Your brother has come, and your father is so happy to have him back safe and sound.' The servant himself seems to be sharing in the great joy of this unexpected return. He respects the family relationships and the person with whom he is speaking by naming one of those inside as 'your brother' and the other as 'your father'. He more or less says to the elder son: 'You too should be delighted that your brother has got back safe and sound.'

But the elder son turns angry, refuses to join the celebration, and sulks outside.

When his father comes out to plead with him, he proves totally self-absorbed. A little highlighting brings this out: 'For all these years I have been working for you, and *I* have never disobeyed your command; yet you have never given *me* even a young goat so that *I* might celebrate with *my* friends.' Then he bitterly refers to his brother not as 'my brother' but as 'this son of yours'. It is an insolent, hateful phrase – one of the most unforgettable sneers in the whole of the New Testament. Self-pity gnaws away at the elder son. He has worked on the property for years, has always been dutiful towards his father, but he has never been given a party like this one! How terrible! He dismisses the welcome-home party as an act of soft and unfair leniency on the part of his father.

The elder son vividly recalls something that I was told years ago when spending time in a house of prayer in California. During my week in that house a group from Alcoholics Anonymous turned up for a course. One of them wandered over to me for a chat before lunch. 'I'm trying to find in the Big

Book,' he told me, 'that place where it says: "Resentment is the number-one killer. It's a luxury we can ill afford."'

Resentment and self-pity fuel the elder son's rage. One need only read the passage aloud to catch the sneering and insulting tone of his voice and words: 'This son of *yours* devoured *your* property with prostitutes.' He almost makes it seem that the father himself has run through his own money in some red-light district, or at least that he has somehow encouraged his younger son to squander everything in bad company.

If the younger son needed to give up a life of wasteful debauchery, the elder son must share his father's feelings of compassion and learn the lesson of love. A cold, unloving, self-righteous sort of person, at heart he is no better than the fellow who took his money and went off to enjoy some high living. To the elder brother are spoken those lovely, appealing words: 'My child, you are always with me, and all that is mine is yours.' The father's meaning is clear: 'You have missed the whole point. Why haven't you been happy? Why can't you love with a tender heart, and join me in joyfully welcoming home your brother? Why have you turned to jealousy and bitterness?'

There the parable breaks off – in a brilliantly open-ended fashion. What happens next? Does the elder brother pull himself together, go inside, and welcome home his younger brother? What does the prodigal son get up to next? Does he help with the farm work but slip out to squander money a few Saturday nights later? Or does he start to behave in a totally acceptable fashion? We don't need to speculate about any aftermath; the story as we have it gives rise to sufficient thought.

In each of us there can be something of both the younger son and his elder brother. We may have strayed away from our Father's home – spiritually, mentally and emotionally. We may have chosen to live our lives elsewhere – in a far country and emotionally estranged from our Father. Or we may have stayed with our Father, but without really enjoying our life with him. We may have done our duty, and done it in a cold, unloving, self-righteous way. But we can always come to ourselves. No matter what our losses have been, we can always repent and return. We can always go in and enjoy our Father's home. We can always rest secure in the thought that he is always with us, and everything he has is ours. Let us explore further the two sons and their presence within each of us.

Various aspects of the story link the two sons. The verb 'to give' offers one subtle link between them. When the younger son worked as a swineherd and suffered the pangs of hunger, he wanted to take some of the pig-food. But no one *gave* him anything. Later on, the elder son complained to his father: 'You have never *given* me even a young goat so that I might celebrate with my friends.' The younger son wanted something given to him so that he might survive, the elder son wanted something given to him so that he might celebrate. Both of them had to learn that their father would give them everything – both to survive and to celebrate. We may have to learn that our God is not only all-powerful and all-knowing but also, and even more, all-giving. It might enrich our prayer to speak that way: 'O all-giving and all-loving God, you let us survive with strength and celebrate with joy.'

Hunger links the two boys as well. The younger son, living away from home in a distant country, dissipates his money and risks starving to death when a famine hits that land. 'I am dying of hunger,' he says to himself. His elder brother, however, suffers from a kind of self-inflicted starvation. He comes back from work in the fields – presumably ravenously hungry and ready for a good meal. Yet his bitter resentment keeps him outside and stops him from enjoying some choice cuts from the fatted calf waiting for him inside. But neither son should go hungry. Their father is lavishly generous, even as God is with us. We never need go hungry.

One of the masterly features in Franco Zeffirelli's *Jesus of Nazareth* was the way he brought together for dramatic effect separate episodes from the life of Christ. He combined, for instance, the feeding of the five thousand with the conversion of Mary Magdalene. A memorable camera-shot picked her out in the crowd as she bit on a hunk of bread before bursting into tears of repentance and joy. With her hands tightly grasping the bread and her moist eyes fixed on Jesus, she knew that her hungry heart had finally found the one who promises: 'Whoever comes to me will never be hungry, and whoever believes in me will never be thirsty' (John 6:35).

The scene from Zeffirelli's film matches perfectly that line from a prize-winning hymn: 'You satisfy the hungry heart.' The line also sums up wonderfully the whole parable of the prodigal son: the father longs to satisfy the hungers of his two sons. He wants to meet their deepest needs, fill their hearts and calm their longings with a peace that will never be taken from them. Servants slip discreetly in and out of Jesus' parable; they are there to serve the father and his family. But who is the true servant in the story? Beyond the shadow of a doubt, the father shows himself to be an exquisite servant. He runs down the road to welcome back the prodigal; he organizes a feast; and then he breaks away from the company to go outside and plead humbly with his elder son. Jesus pictures God as a perfectly loving father who does everything to serve, with incredible tact and delicacy, his two difficult sons.

A TALE OF GOD'S LOVE

This last thought clearly shifts the focus away from the two sons and back to the heart of the parable: the father's love. Let us prayerfully reflect further on three characteristics of that love.

A Supremely Free Act

First of all, in general, mere reason can never fully account for the choices and the intensity of true love. Of course, love, wherever we see it in action, is never simply unmotivated. We can always point to reasons that help to explain, for instance, loving relationships with our marriage partner or our friends. But by themselves rational motives can never completely explain and justify love, what it chooses and what it does. Being a supremely free act, love is always gratuitous and never compelled. It is a mysterious act of freedom which is never forced or simply controlled by other factors – not even by the force of reason. To be sure, we run up against a real mystery here. How can a loving action be rational and yet not be fully clarified or justified by reason alone? What happens when love leads someone to do things that go beyond the merely reasonable?

In the case of the father in Jesus' parable, sheer reason fails to account fully for his actions. After all, he could have imposed conditions on his runaway son. He might have required him to work for several years as a hired hand before accepting him back into the family circle. When told that the elder son was sulking aside, he might have stayed inside with the comment: 'He'll get over his bad mood. The smell of the veal will bring him inside.' Undoubtedly one can and should recall his parental relationship. These two brothers are his sons, and nothing anyone does can change that fact. But this uniquely loving father goes well beyond what modern society would propose as the reasonable, mature reactions of a parent to their misbehaviour, and certainly far beyond anything that might have been expected from a wealthy father in the patriarchal society of Jesus' time. The father in the parable is wonderfully free in the delicate ways he shows his love towards his sons. He reaches out with a unique compassion to both of them. Merely reasonable motives cannot justify what he does, just as mere reason can never explain the intensity and mysterious freedom with which God loves all of us.

To be sure, one might well recall that we are made in God's image and likeness (Genesis 1:26–7). God sees in us, one may say, divine icons. But why does God pursue us with such lavish love when we run away from home or sulk bitterly outside?

Surely enough is enough? Yet, despite our horrendous sins or even more mysteriously because of them, God reaches out in love to each one of us. God is never irrational. Yet the divine heart has its reasons that seem to go far beyond anything we might rationally justify.

There is more than an edge of mystery when we attempt to answer the question: Why did God create us to begin with? It was and is a mysterious act of divine freedom to create and then to sustain in existence, from moment to moment, all things that have been created. All the more, we cannot account in a merely rational way for the greater mystery of God's love in reaching out to dissolute, ungrateful and embittered sinners.

Reason and Love

Our first point has brought up the way love, while not irrational, goes beyond the merely reasonable. But we need, second, to think a little about the interplay of reason and love. This interplay is admittedly mysterious but it may also help to illuminate something of the prodigal son story.

A modern prejudice holds that love distorts things, inevitably prevents lovers from understanding the reality of the beloved, is essentially deceptive, and necessarily produces false idealizations based on fantasy. In *A Midsummer Night's Dream* William Shakespeare presents love as fostering illusions, seeing beauty that is not there, and leading us away from the real world. At the start of the final act, when Theseus equates lovers with poets *and madmen*, one is left wondering how the 'seething brains' of lovers can apprehend anything of reality. In a later play (*As You Like It*) Shakespeare has Rosalind dismiss love for being 'merely a madness' (3.2.420). In a word, love is supposed to be blind or even worse.

Undoubtedly, passionate, romantic love can lead some people astray and intoxicate them into 'seeing' what is not there. But otherwise Shakespeare's view of things seems, alas, to be rather befuddled and runs clean contrary to the link that John's

Gospel, St Augustine of Hippo, William of Saint Thierry, St Thomas Aquinas and many others have recognized between knowing and loving. His special love allows the beloved disciple to leap to the truth about the resurrection (John 20:8) and later to identify the mysterious stranger standing on the beach at dawn (John 21:7). 'Show me a lover and he will understand,' St Augustine exclaimed when commenting on John's Gospel (26.4). In *The Nature and Dignity of Love*, William of Saint Thierry championed the role of love as enlightening reason and making reality intelligible (e.g. 15, 21). Commenting on the second book of Peter Lombard's *Sentences*, Aquinas left us the lapidary observation: 'Where there is love, there is vision.' Great voices from the Christian tradition argue that the eyes of love let us see, whereas the eyes of hatred are sure to lead us astray. In short, it is hatred rather than love that is blind. Love between persons opens the way to knowledge and recognizing real values in the beloved, even if it may disapprove of some deficient characteristics.

Let me apply love's insight to the case in hand. The loving father in the parable of the prodigal son is only too painfully aware of the sinful situation of his younger boy. But love makes him also aware of his potentialities for growth – a point lost on the elder son who is bitter about his sibling and can see nothing good in him. Jesus' parable not only evokes the truth seen by the merciful eyes of divine love but also rings true in common human experience. Those who love perceive the meaning and truth in people and things; love enables us to see meaning and catch sight of truth. In love with us, God knows what we can become through the grace bestowed on us, just as the father in the parable knows the deep goodness of his two sons and the greatness into which they might grow. He sees with his heart, and cherishes each of them as incomparably unique and utterly special individuals.

The Risk of Love

The last characteristic of love that emerges from Jesus' parable is the way love exposes one to suffering. Love never sponsors the active aggression suggested by the words of a once-popular song, 'You always hurt the one you love'. It is quite the contrary: real love produces vulnerability and sends lovers out over open ground under fire. In the Middle Ages the exponents of courtly love, whether found in fiction or practised in real life, certainly appreciated the suffering and risk of suffering that love entails, especially when the lover is separated from the beloved. Generous, self-sacrificing and unconditional love risks being exploited, rejected and even murderously crushed.

Loving service to those in terrible need can turn one into a target. The last few decades have seen thousands of good Samaritans paying with their lives because they stopped for wounded travellers. In less dramatic but very real ways, those who love constantly make themselves vulnerable by reaching out in their concern for others.

No parable from the Gospels summons up more poignantly the risk of love than the story of the merciful father. He first runs down the road to greet his younger son, and later leaves the banquet to plead with his elder son. His love leads him to face and endure the insulting behaviour of his elder son, as well as deep pain over the moral and spiritual death of his younger son. One does not need to strain to hear the sorrow in his words about his son who has been 'lost' and 'dead'. The father's love creates his way of the cross or 'passion'.

In various languages a wise choice calls Jesus' suffering and death his 'passion' – a term that combines intense love with the mortal suffering it brought our divine Lover. The passion stories in the Gospels track the steadfastness of Jesus' loving commitment that made him vulnerable right to the end. His self- forgetful love exposes him to atrocious suffering and death. The greatest of Jesus' parables more than hints at the 'passion' which the father risks and endures precisely because of his utterly generous love towards his two sons. Love makes God vulnerable, as we see when we gaze at the figure on the cross.

In Jesus' parable of the prodigal son the father's love drives him to do what mere reason cannot justify. He sees his two sons with the heart, and accepts the risks involved in reaching out to them. The younger son returns home and accepts his father's loving welcome. The father also holds out a hand in love to his elder son. But that point the parable breaks off – a challenge to Jesus' original audience and to all subsequent Christians. Will the elder son and will we accept the love God offers us?

A PRAYER

> O all-good God, you know me and you love me far more than I know and love myself.
> I cast myself into the arms of your infinite love,
> and entrust to you my whole life, with all its joys, sorrows, successes and failures.
> Deal with me as you know best, and keep me always safe at home with you,
> my ever-living and ever-loving God.

EXERCISES

1 Try acting out with three friends the entire parable of the prodigal son. One person plays the father, another the younger son, a third a servant, and a fourth the elder brother.

2 What do you think happens between the two brothers once the action of the parable ends?

3 What changes would you make if you transposed the parable and made it into a story of a mother and her two daughters?

4 In the parable the father says to the elder son: 'Child, you
  are always with me, and all that is mine is yours.' Do you
  find any parallel in what St Paul writes: 'All things belong
  to you, and you belong to Christ, and Christ belongs to
  God' (1 Corinthians 3:22–3)?

THE LABOURERS IN
THE VINEYARD

The kingdom of heaven is like a landowner who went out early in the morning to hire labourers for his vineyard. After agreeing with the labourers for the usual daily wage, he sent them into his vineyard. When he went out about nine o'clock, he saw others standing idle in the marketplace; and he said to them, 'You also go into the vineyard, and I will pay you whatever is right.' So they went. When he went out again about noon and about three o'clock, he did the same. And about five o'clock he went out and found others standing around; and he said to them, 'Why are you standing here idle all day?' They said to him, 'Because no one has hired us.' He said to them, 'You also go into the vineyard.' When evening came, the owner of the vineyard said to his manager, 'Call the labourers and give them their pay, beginning with the last and then going to the first.' When those hired about five o'clock came, each of them received the usual daily wage. Now when the first came, they thought they would receive more; but each of them also received the usual daily wage. And when they received it, they grumbled against the landowner, saying, 'These last worked only one hour, and you have made them equal to us who have borne the burden of the day and the scorching heat.' But he replied to one of them, 'Friend, I am doing you no wrong. Did you not agree with me for the usual daily wage? Take what belongs to you and go; I choose to give to this last the same as I give to you. Am I not allowed to do what I choose with what belongs to me? Or are you envious because I am generous?'

(Matthew 20:1–15)

Located in a public marketplace and a privately owned vineyard, this parable features an employer, a silent manager, and
five groups of unskilled labourers whom the owner hires – presumably at the time of grape harvest: one group early in the
morning, another around nine, a third at midday, a fourth at
three in the afternoon and a fifth an hour before sunset. The
reference to the 'scorching heat' makes one think of an un-
usually hot autumn day, with perhaps a storm coming up. By
listing the hours from six a.m. ('early morning') through to six
p.m. ('evening'), the parable conveys the feeling of the hard
working day grinding past slowly.

We find this parable only in Matthew's Gospel, just as we
find that of the prodigal son only in Luke's Gospel. They are
not totally equivalent: the father of the prodigal does not, for
instance, offer a self-description, as does the landowner ('I am
generous'). Yet the two parables match each other in bringing
out how different our God is from what we might expect.[1] In
particular, the remarkable generosity of Matthew's landowner
confronts any tendency in us to sympathize with the viewpoint
of those who have laboured all day and of the elder brother
in Luke's parable. Is our God selectively generous with those
whom we do not see as particularly deserving? Surely God
should follow the good old rule of 'equal pay for equal work', or
rather, 'more pay for more work'?

The two parables match each other also in the discreet way
they bring in God. On the face of it both are very human, this-
worldly stories. That of the prodigal son gives an account of a
father's painful difficulties with his two sons; the story of the
labourers in the vineyard pictures a problem of labour relations
in an agricultural setting. God turns up in the guise of a reverent equivalent when the prodigal son first rehearses and then
delivers his brief speech: 'Father, I have sinned against heaven
and before you.' Jesus introduces the other parable with a similar reverent circumlocution for God: 'The kingdom of heaven
is like ...' Despite the worldly tone of both stories, each of

them deftly refers to our heavenly Father and is concerned to answer the question: What is our God like? With superb tact, Jesus guides us spiritually and initiates us into the mystery of God, by telling these stories that we must mull over if we are going to get the point and let God take over in our lives. Here as elsewhere, Jesus does a major part of his spiritual direction through being a story-teller.

A NASTY SCENE

The parable of the labourers in the vineyard opens with a normal, labour-intensive situation, one that still turns up year by year around the world. Owners of vineyards need extra workers at the time of harvest. In some countries you can still see such day-labourers lining up at dawn. In Italy we call these workmen *braccianti*, or hired hands; they roll up their sleeves and bare their *braccia*, or arms, in what they are hired to do. An old Italian adage speaks of '*tanto lavoro e così poche braccia* (such a lot of work and so few hands)'. The parable ends, if only in part, with a normal scene: the casual labourers receive their pay, a denarius ('the usual daily wage') at nightfall. Ordinary justice demands (and demanded) that such day-workers be paid when night comes. The Book of Leviticus prescribed just that· 'You shall not keep for yourself the wages of a labourer until morning' (19:13).

Some Strange Twists

After an unsurprising opening, Jesus quickly gives the story some strange twists. Why doesn't the owner hire a full crew early in the morning, around six o'clock, and then stay around with them in the vineyard while they stay on the job all day and complete the harvest? It is particularly puzzling that he needs extra hands at five o'clock in the afternoon, just an hour or so before sunset.[2] Has a threatening storm started to blow up? Or does the landowner enjoy the use of grape-crushing facilities only for a day and the harvest is proving bigger than he first expected? Or does he plan to go elsewhere the following day and has found that he miscalculated the number of workers he needs for a bumper harvest?

It is also, to say the least, a bit baffling that some day-labourers are still there at five in the afternoon. One could imagine them hanging on and waiting for some work up to midday or a little later. But one would think that everyone would have given up and cleared off by late afternoon – just an hour before sunset. It is surprising to find them still there and waiting patiently for someone to hire them. Who is going to engage workers for only one hour?

Some scholars who comment on this parable tell us that those 'others' whom the landowner finds at nine o'clock, noon, three o'clock and five o'clock had not been there earlier. Well, where were they, if the landowner didn't find them at the labour exchange in the central marketplace earlier in the day? Had they been sleeping in? Or doing some part-time jobs else-where during the morning? Or had they been waiting around in the marketplace of another town or village and had given up looking for work there? Some reader is sure to write and tell me that I should suspend my disbelief and not ask such questions. But I would still like to know what those day-labourers who were hired very late had been up to earlier in the day. A lame alternative explanation would be that the landowner simply didn't notice them standing in the line when he first rushed into the marketplace.

If They Win, I Lose

Jesus, so it seems, is already loosening up his audience by taking them beyond ordinary human situations and preparing them for the dramatic puzzle to come when they hear about two extraordinary decisions made by the landowner at the end of the day. To begin with, why doesn't he tell his manager to pay first those who have been hired first and who worked on the harvest right through the day? They could take their wages, head home and not be forced to wait around to see how fantastically generous the landowner is going to be with the workers who signed on at the last hour. It would be so easy to avoid any grumbling, bitter complaints about unfair treatment, and the ugly scene at the end of the day. The order one might have expected for paying the labourers would have meant a peaceful closure to the story. Those who have worked for only one hour surely would not mind being paid last. Then they would have been quite surprised and utterly delighted to receive a full day's wage. Giving three cheers for their wonderfully generous employer, they would have disappeared into the night.

Instead, the landowner seems deliberately provocative, both with his first decision to put those hired last at the head of the pay queue and even more with his second decision to be outrageously generous with those who have worked so little. That second decision is simply bewildering. He challenges normal views about proper rights and rewards. His selective generosity undermines our normal human system of just rewards. To put it mildly, Jesus' story challenges our usual notions of fairness.

Those who have worked in the vineyard all day bring to mind everyone who sees life as a competition and moves forward in the spirit of 'if they win, I lose'. Such a competitive spirit fosters the constant need to compare ourselves with 'those others', especially with those 'undeserving' others. My successes or failures over against 'them' provide the basis for my self-evaluation and self-image. Like the elder brother in the story of the prodigal son and the labourers who have worked through the day, we can too easily take life as a competition in which we fail or succeed. Do I feel myself a failed competitor when others are treated with extraordinary generosity?

Jesus puts his finger squarely on a pervasive meanness of spirit that is not limited to workers who don't like seeing others treated with special generosity. The indignation of the men in the parable calls to mind what the elder brother of the prodigal son says in complaint: 'I have worked well and faithfully all these years. And what has this disgraceful son of yours got up to in his life of dissipation!' The labourers in the vineyard complain, precisely because they 'have borne the burden of the day and the scorching heat', and not because the last comers have proved themselves incompetent slackers or have been stealing on the job. This is to forget the misery of those who have waited desperately all day for the chance of making a little money from some casual work. In their own way, the men hired at five o'clock have been bearing the burden of the day and the scorching heat before they surprisingly get a chance of earning something. Those who have worked through the day ignore all that, just as the elder brother fails to think of the suffering his sinful younger brother has been through. Those who complain in both parables show a certain meanness of spirit, an insistence on matters of justice and principle that cannot cope with acts of extraordinary mercy shown by the owner and the father, respectively.

OUR GENEROUS GOD

In his story of the labourers in the vineyard Jesus wants to let us see how large-minded our God is. God is recklessly generous, wonderfully loving and completely different from anything that we might expect. Jesus certainly does not offer us the picture of God that we may very well anticipate or even want: God as strictly democratic, scrupulously fair and quite predictable. Like the landowner in the parable, God is the opposite: a God of surprises.

A Universe of Rigid Equality

Imagine for a moment a universe run on the principle of rigid equality. Make a mental experiment and think of a world in which everyone was equally beautiful, equally healthy and equally intelligent. We would all win exactly the same prizes in life's lottery. No accidents of history or geography would make any difference to what each of us would receive. Everything would be strictly egalitarian – in terms of the talents distributed and the chances each one is given.

Whatever anyone might say to recommend such an imaginary utopia, it's not the world we know and it doesn't fit the parable Jesus tells us. Jesus' God is fair to all, just as the landowner does no one any wrong but pays everyone the daily wage they had agreed to. God certainly does no one any wrong and yet is not equal with all, inasmuch as God is infinitely free, creative and unimaginably kind. God is never unjust and yet treats everyone in an unpredictable, endlessly variable range of ways, because God takes each of us as uniquely special and simply irreplaceably valuable individuals. Whether or not we complain and grumble, God calls each of us 'my friend'.

Years ago a spiritual director managed to irritate me regularly when he came to my college every month and addressed me and other seminarians preparing to be ordained priests. No matter what topic he had chosen, he managed to insert with great gusto a line God delivers in the Book of Isaiah: ' "My thoughts are not your thoughts, nor are your ways my ways," says the Lord' (55:8). I fell into the habit of waiting for that line and not paying attention to anything else the priest was saying. But how right he was! After all these years I can see that he valued something very special about God. It was something that the landowner in Jesus' parable of the labourers in the vineyard could well have said to the grumblers: 'My ways are not your ways.'

Jesus does his best in this parable to convince us that we shouldn't judge our lives or the lives of others in terms of performance. Ultimately it doesn't make any difference whether we work through a complete daytime or lifetime of public success, or simply get taken on at five o'clock in the afternoon. What matters for all of us is the reckless generosity and exuberant kindness of God.

All is Grace

Everything and everyone belongs to God. Our God does what he chooses with what is his, and he always chooses with an infinite inventiveness and overflowing goodness. No modern writer has caught more powerfully the sense that our lives and destiny, no matter how strangely unequal and painfully unsuccessful they seem, are sheer gift from God than Georges Bernanos in *The Diary of a Country Priest*.

The novel repeatedly returns to the same question: What is the basis for our life in the presence of God? How should we interpret our existence in the vineyard in which we work? A young French priest confides to his diary his experiences in a country parish:

My parish is bored stiff, no other word for it. Like so many others! We can see them being eaten up with boredom, and we can't do anything about it. Someday perhaps we shall catch it ourselves – become aware of the cancerous growth within us. You can keep going a long time with that in you.[3]

With simplicity and candour he describes the hopes he entertains and the problems and disappointments he meets in his work for the community and in his contacts with his fellow priests. Physically he suffers a great deal. He burns himself out and eventually will die of stomach cancer.

Along the way the young priest has a dramatic conversation with the local countess. She lost her son when he was eighteen months old; she hates her daughter; her husband has proved unfaithful. Her sufferings have made her bitter. When the countess confesses her bitterness and hatred, the young priest says to her: 'God is not to be bargained with. We must give ourselves up to God unconditionally.' But why should the countess or anyone else follow the priest's advice to 'give everything'?

The answer comes through powerfully at the end of *The Diary of a Country Priest*. It is because God has first graced us with everything that we owe God everything in return. The whole of our existence is a free gift made by God, who is utterly free and totally loving. The novel closes when the young priest, already desperately ill from cancer, goes to visit an old school-friend who persuades him to stop overnight. Next morning his host discovers the priest vomiting great quantities of blood. He describes what follows:

The haemorrhage subsided. While I was waiting for the doctor, our friend regained consciousness. Yet he did not speak. Great beads of perspiration were rolling over his brow and cheeks. His eyes, which I could scarcely see under his heavy, half-closed lids, told of great pain. I felt his pulse and it was rapidly growing weak. A young neighbour went to fetch our parish priest...

The priest was still on the way. I felt bound to express to my unfortunate comrade my deep regret that such delay threatened to deprive him of the final consolations of the Church. He did not seem to hear me. But a few minutes later he put his hand over mine, and his eyes entreated me to draw closer to him. He then uttered these words almost in my ear. And I am quite sure that I have recorded them accurately, for his voice, though halting, was strangely distinct. 'What does it matter? All is grace.' I think he died just then.[4]

Through his novel Bernanos articulates brilliantly that message, which is nothing else than the message of Jesus: all is gift from God. We never have the right to complain or grumble that we are treated badly or that others are being treated better. God does with us what he wills, and what God wills is always for our lasting good.

A PRAYER

O God of boundless freedom and generosity,
Take away from our hearts all grumbling and envy.
Do what you choose with us and with our world, which
    is your world.
We thank you for all your gifts and graces,
and we trust that in your will is our peace.

EXERCISES

1 What·are the inequalities in your life that tempt you to complain?
2 When you look back, do some inequalities and injustices now appear to be great blessings?
3 Try a little grumbling in your prayer, and see whether you find God talking with you as 'my friend'.

1 In *A Reading of the Parables* (London: Darton, Longman & Todd, 1998) Ruth Etchells notes how both parables include
  'the worthy and the hardworking, who have proper and formal expectations of what is publicly, even legally, regarded as the proper reward for their toil. In both there is someone who has not deserved, under such an agreed system of rewards, anything much. And in both there is a central figure who, apart from any natural emotional bonding, is in a formal legal relationship which has contractual dimensions either as parent or as employer, with all the others; who from his own wealth chooses to honour the terms of the contract with the worthy, but to go far beyond it in generosity to the unworthy. In both, this person is challenged angrily by those who seem merely to have received their "due". In both, the reply of the central figure to his challengers indicates a way of perceiving the situation, and its needs, wholly other than the fiercely exacting "justice" or "fairness" being pressed upon him.' (p. 25)
2 It is a lovely touch when Jesus expresses the owner's concern for the disheartened men who are still waiting to be hired at five p.m.: 'Why are you standing here?' For them it is now or never; otherwise they will not share

in the harvest, which hints fairly clearly at the abundant harvest of God's coming kingdom.

3 G. Bernanos, *The Diary of a Country Priest*, trans. P. Morris (London: Boriswood, 1937), p. 9.

4 Ibid., pp. 316–17; translation corrected.

CHAPTER FOUR

GROWTH AND LIFE

The kingdom of God is as if someone would scatter seed on the ground, and would sleep and rise night and day, and the seed would sprout and grow, he does not know how. The earth produces of itself, first the stalk, then the head, then the full grain in the head. But when the grain is ripe, at once he goes in with his sickle, because the harvest has come…

With what can we compare the kingdom of God, or what parable will we use for it? It is like a mustard seed, which, when sown upon the ground, is the smallest of all the seeds on earth; yet when it is sown it grows up and becomes the greatest of all shrubs, and puts forth large branches, so that the birds of the air can make nests in its shade.

(Mark 4:26–32)

One of life's special blessings for me was the chance of growing up on a farm. Those years taught me the lesson of marvelling at the mystery of new life: fluffy chickens darting ahead of the hens, white rings of flowers on the pear trees, wild rabbits enjoying the grass on an early summer's evening. I still feel a thrill of wonder when I remember all that growth: cows licking their newborn calves, sharp-eyed magpies strutting around with their young, and – not least – peas and beans shooting up through soil where I had planted seeds in the vegetable garden.

IMAGES FROM FARMING

Once I started to read the Gospels seriously, it made me happy to find how often Jesus draws his images from farming. He knows that donkeys and oxen need to be taken every day to drink water (Luke 13:15). These animals may at times fall down wells and must be rescued even on the sacred day of rest (Luke 14:5; Matthew 12:11). Jesus recalls how barren fig trees might be revitalized by cultivating the soil and adding some fertilizer (Luke 13:8). He has learnt how to predict the weather. Winds from the west blow off the Mediterranean and bring rain; those from the south come off the desert and will be hot and dry (Luke 12:54–5). He knows that farmers might buy up to five yoke of oxen (Luke 14:19), and that Gentiles feed pigs on pods. Piling up manure heaps (Luke 14:35), growing mulberry trees (Luke 17:6), minding sheep, ploughing the land – references to these and other farming activities dot the preaching of Jesus.

The marvel of seeds that send up shoots and slowly but surely produce crops and trees really caught his eye. He drew on these agricultural experiences to make up parables that speak to us of God's powerful rule establishing itself in our world. Where the story of the prodigal son expressed the merciful love of God and the story of the labourers in the vineyard the divine freedom which we dare not challenge, Jesus' parables of growth encouraged an utter confidence in God's power to bring about the new and wonderful life of the final kingdom. Many good things of the kingdom are happening right now, and many more are on the way. The kingdom of God will carry all before it.

There is a lovely homeliness to these parables of growth. Where the Old Testament knew God to be even more powerful than the majestic cedars of Lebanon (Isaiah 2:13), Jesus brings divine things right down to earth: to grains of wheat and tiny mustard seeds. It is all rather like what he does by turning eagles into barnyard hens. The Old Testament compared God's care for the chosen people to the magnificent flight of an eagle carrying its young. Jesus knows these images but prefers to picture himself as a barnyard hen with her chickens. 'How often,' he exclaims, 'have I desired to gather your children together as a hen gathers her brood under her wings, and you were not willing' (Luke 13:34). Just as God nurtures and protects us in homely ways, so the divine power works in all the growth and life that surrounds us. Jesus wants us to look at our gardens, our orchards and our fields. Quietly but powerfully God makes everything grow and bloom and ripen – a plain and unpretentious picture of how he wants to share with everyone life in lasting abundance.

Jesus, I believe, would have delighted in a natural phenomenon which occurs every few years in the centre of Australia. A monsoon swings off course and dumps tonnes of water across the dry desert land. Within a few weeks, under the blazing sun, plants spring up, flowers bloom, birds return, and the deep mud below previously dried-up lakes produces fish. The 'dead heart' comes alive. 'What a shame you couldn't stay on!' I told a Danish student who visited me recently in Rome. When talking about my views on the Holy Trinity, she discovered that I am Australian and mentioned a visit she had made some years ago to Alice Springs. 'When we flew into the centre,' she recalled, 'it rained steadily for days. We couldn't climb Ayer's Rock; waterfalls were cascading down its slopes.' What can happen to the 'dead heart' of Australia highlights in a startling fashion the life and growth that God gives everywhere: in ancient Galilee, over the hills of modern Somerset, and across the plains of Iowa.

LIFE ABUNDANTLY

Years ago over the Christmas break in Rome I went to the Capitoline Museum for a fascinating exhibition called 'Andy Warhol versus Giorgio de Chirico'. It displayed works by de Chirico alongside versions of them painted by Warhol. Before going to the exhibition, I borrowed the catalogue from a friend. When I began browsing through it, a fascinating interview with Warhol set off all kinds of thoughts in my head. Among other things, he pleaded strongly for the notable significance of contemporary advertising: 'Even when I watch television, I like the advertising better than the film or the programme being shown ... I view advertising as an artistic expression of our times. I watch advertising just as much as I go to museums.' They were not surprising sentiments from someone who created art out of conglomerates of soup tins and bottles of Coca-Cola.

Nevertheless, the interview sounded challenging and even provocative. Hence, after visiting the Capitoline Museum for 'Andy Warhol versus Giorgio de Chirico', I started checking billboards around the city and examining advertisements at stations in the Roman underground system. What instantly struck me was how often the advertising promised to enhance our life. One brand of Parmesan cheese offered to help customers to 'live in good form and live better'. A huge advertisement for milk guaranteed to help milk-drinkers towards a 'better life (*tanto latte per vivere meglio*)'. One brand of bitter liqueur (Amaro) played on its name to assure prospective drinkers that it would 'make life less bitter'. An unsweetened Riesling wine simply held out 'the pleasures of life'. To encourage more citizens to take part in the marathon at New Year, the city administration had put out huge banners urging Romans to 'live sport (*viviamo lo sport*)'. A political party was running its national meeting under a slogan that stressed its point by joining the verb and the noun: 'to live life (*per vivere la vita*)'. Not unexpectedly, the latest copy of *Playboy* magazine was selling itself under the caption of 'all the pleasures of life'.

The results intrigued me when I took Warhol's advice and checked some of Rome's advertising. All that publicity for food, drink, sport, political engagement and uncommitted sex promised customers a richer, more satisfying life. Whatever the value of the particular items being promoted and whatever the artistic

merits or demerits of the advertisements themselves, the messages all converged on one magic word: life. They all undertook
to enhance and improve human life. Eat this cheese and drink
this Riesling or somehow fail to live. Be a consumer or miss out
on what matters. Be a playboy or be nothing.

When I reflected on all these advertisements, my mind
went back to an earlier age: to Jesus' own message of growth
and life and to what happened to that message after he died and
rose from the dead. Some of his most unforgettable parables
took up very ordinary farming experiences and coaxed or even
pushed us into thinking about God's power in bringing life and
growth. 'Be a member of this new reign of God,' he was imply-
ing, 'or miss out on what matters and fail to live. Be part of this
final kingdom or be nothing.' When they experienced the risen
Jesus and his Spirit, early Christians knew him to be Life itself.
Jesus had preached his message of the new life of the divine
kingdom; now they knew him to be that Life in person. The
First Letter of John opened by saying just that:

We declare to you what was from the beginning, what we have
heard, what we have seen with our eyes, what we have looked at
and touched with our hands, concerning the *Word of Life* – this
Life was revealed, and we have seen it and testify to it, and
declare to you *the eternal Life* that was with the Father and was
revealed to us.

(1 John 1:1–2)

Many scholars have accurately expressed the shift from the
period of Jesus' own preaching to the time of the emerging
Church by saying: 'The Preacher became the One who was
preached.' To say the least, the Preacher of life and growth
came to be known and followed as the very source of growth,
even Life itself.[1]

John's Gospel, while not including any of the parables
Jesus preached, vigorously puts across their meaning for those

who join the Church as the first century goes on. This Gospel
does just that for the parables of growth by identifying the risen
Christ as Life itself. The theme runs from John's prologue, 'in
him was life' (John 1:3), through the promise, 'I came that they
may have life and have it abundantly' (John 10:10), to the stag-
gering self-descriptions that come from Jesus: 'I am the resurrection and the life' (John 11:25); 'I am the way, and the truth,
and the life' (John 14:6). Just in case any reader may have read
the text but missed the meaning, the Gospel ends by clearly
stating its intention: 'These things are written so that you may
come to believe that Jesus is the Messiah, the Son of God, and
that through believing you may have *life* in his name' (John
20:31).

Reading advertisements in Rome, mulling over Jesus' parables of growth, and rereading John's Gospel confronted me
with two very different messages about life and also reminded
me of the two biblical words for life. English, Italian, German
and a number of other languages have only one word: 'life',
vita, *Leben*, and so forth. The New Testament, however, was
written in Greek and has two words: *zoe* (which is connected
with zoology or the scientific study of animals) and *bios* (which
we find taken into many current English words like biochem-
istry, bio-ethics, and biology, or the science of life). John's
Gospel and the First Letter of John use *zoe* in the passages
quoted above and elsewhere. Jesus promises, for instance, *zoe*
and not *bios*; he identifies himself with *zoe* and not with *bios*.
What's the difference between the two words? What's so special
about *zoe* or life in St John's sense?

One should admit that life in any sense is marvellous, elu-
sive, and impossible to pin down and define totally. There's
something true about the sentiment expressed in the old love
song: 'O sweet mystery of life'. To be sure, scientists have discovered an enormous amount about matters biological and
zoological. Yet there is still much more to know. We don't, for
instance, have a convincing theory to account for the origin of

life on earth. It's still anybody's guess how terrestrial life first appeared, let alone whether there is life elsewhere in the universe and, if so, how those alien, extraterrestrial life-forms emerged.

But St John, like lovers everywhere, talks not of life which comes through things when the conditions are right, but of the life we experience and receive through persons – the *zoe* or life for ever that personal faith in Jesus brings. It's no accident that the First Letter of John begins by witnessing to experience: to the One who has been heard, seen, looked upon and touched. It is personal experience of Jesus that proves life-giving. To experience Jesus is to experience the One who gives life 'abundantly' and proves himself the very 'bread of life'.

When preaching his parables and even more when risen from the dead, Jesus was and is well within reach – for us to experience him in common and accept him together. During his earthly ministry Jesus preached publicly; his parables encouraged all his hearers to let the power of God's kingdom bring them growth. After the resurrection the First Letter of John testified to what 'we' have experienced and continue to experienced together. Accepting the crucified and risen Jesus means passing 'from death to life' (1 John 3:14). The *zoe*, to which this letter and John's Gospel witnessed, is an amazing new life in common: a life to be experienced, shared and proclaimed together.

LIFE THROUGH DEATH

This growth and life come not only together but also through death. Dying is the way to this new living. John's Gospel may well be echoing and developing Jesus' parables about growing seeds when we hear Jesus say: 'Unless a grain of wheat falls into the earth and dies, it remains just a single grain; but if it dies, it bears much fruit' (John 12:24). Jesus saw the power of God's coming kingdom in the seed that is buried in the ground and

sends fresh life sprouting up. The preacher of the seed dramatizes his own parable by dying and being buried to bring forth
the richest of harvests.

Repeatedly, John's Gospel indicates such death as the way
to life. When Jesus promises life 'abundantly', the very next
verse identifies him as the 'good shepherd' who dies for his
sheep (John 10:11). In proving himself 'the resurrection and
the life' by raising Lazarus from the dead, Jesus provokes his
enemies into plotting his death (John 11:45–53). When he calls
himself 'the way, and the truth, and the life', Jesus is spending
his last evening with the core group of his friends. Over and
over again in that final discourse (John 13–17) we read of the
death which Jesus is ready to face – for them and for us. To
be a life-giver and a harvest-maker, he will become like a
grain of wheat falling into the ground and dying. At the end
Jesus acts out what he has preached in his parables about seed
being sown.

Life is a magic word; it is something everyone hungers
for. Audiences everywhere resonated with the cry 'To life!' in
Fiddler on the Roof. When Andy Warhol sent me off to study
Roman billboards and advertisements in the underground,
those 'artistic expressions of our times' reminded me vividly of
how we all yearn for the fullness of life. At the same time, Jesus'
preaching and John's Gospel show us that life is more than *bios*;
it's *zoe*. Genuine life is not there for the taking or the making,
as modern advertising and *Playboy* magazine would have it – in
the spirit of 'here's life, help yourself'. We don't live by helping
ourselves to things and exploiting others, but by truly experi-
encing persons, above all the person of Jesus himself. Real life
does not come by taking it for ourselves but by receiving it
from him and sharing it with others.

When we remember how Jesus himself became a life-giver
and harvest-maker by passing through death, those who receive
life from him are themselves called to go the same way. What
was true of Jesus touches all his followers: 'Unless a grain of

wheat falls into the earth and dies, it remains just a single grain; but if it dies, it bears much fruit.'

A STARTLING CONTRAST

The parables Jesus draws from grain seeds and mustard seeds are stories of a growth that is beyond our understanding and control. These stories encourage us to open our eyes to the divine energy that is at work in our world. They take me back to my childhood and how I would dart out in the freshness of the morning to find that shoots were sprouting out through the soil where I had planted seeds in the vegetable garden. Some days later rows of beans and peas stood up cheerfully in the sunlight. Vital energy was at work, even though I did not know how. God was already offering me a lesson of how the growth and fruitful increase of the divine kingdom goes beyond our understanding and control.

That lesson was driven home years later and in another part of the world. In 1977 I spent a month of prayer in California, spending the first week in a house in Azusa. Around one million trees and shrubs were growing in the Monrovia Nursery that surrounded that house of prayer. Some were already ten or twelve feet high; other plants were so far only a few inches high. But all of them received water every day and were growing away furiously under the sun. The nursery offered its own powerful image of the fruitful growth of God's kingdom.

Through these parables Jesus gently encourages us to realize a startling contrast in the history of God's kingdom: between its small and unpromising beginning and its huge outcome in the future. A minute mustard seed, the size of a pinhead, seems only a tiny, inconspicuous start. Yet the mysterious, dynamic power at work will bring a great and glorious ending, imaged forth by a mustard tree which is large enough to shelter the nests of birds. Overwhelming results will arise from a very humble start. Jesus sets himself to open up a vision of the divine force at work in our world; he knows with an utter assurance that a wonderful, enormous ending will come.

The scriptures that Jesus prayed over use the image of a sheltering tree. Ezekiel, for instance, imagines God taking 'a sprig from the lofty top of a cedar' and planting it 'on a high and lofty mountain' where it will become 'a noble cedar'. Then 'under it every kind of bird will live; in the shade of its branches will nest winged creatures of every kind' (Ezekiel 17:22–3). By contrast, Jesus' picture is modest and homely: a tiny mustard seed that will become a bushy, welcoming shrub at the bottom of the garden.

Once again we profit by observing how Jesus himself acted out his own parables. He was and is the divine kingdom in person. Dying and being buried in the ground like a tiny mustard seed, he rose from the dead to trigger the startling growth of a world-wide community and to touch the lives of millions who have not joined that community through baptism. The tree of the cross, as many believers have imaginatively grasped, became a living tree with branches large enough to shelter the whole of the human race. The crucified and risen Jesus himself is the minute mustard seed that has grown to welcome and shelter the world.

The Book of Daniel portrays a huge world-tree which stands at the centre of the earth, reaches to the heavens, and shelters all life:

There was a tree at the centre of the earth, and its height was great. The tree grew great and strong, its top reached to heaven, and it was visible to the ends of the whole earth. Its foliage was beautiful, its fruit abundant, and it provided food for all. The animals of the field found shade under it, the birds of the air nested in its branches, and from it all living beings were fed.

(Daniel 4:10–12)

But in the prophetic vision this world-tree is cut down, its branches chopped down, and its foliage stripped away. The tragic tree symbolizes the unfortunate king of Babylon, Nebuchadnezzar (Daniel 4:22). Where he failed to become a lasting haven even for his own people, the cross of Jesus will give shelter and life to all human beings.

THE GIFT BECOMES A RESPONSIBILITY

Jesus acted out his own parables of growth and turned them into a testing invitation for his followers. Will they play their part in harvesting the growth which the power of the kingdom brings? Moved to pity by the sight of crowds of people who seemed helpless and harassed like sheep without a shepherd, Jesus said to his disciples: 'The harvest is plentiful but the labourers are few; therefore ask the Lord of the harvest to send out labourers into the harvest' (Matthew 9:37–8). John's Gospel develops this theme when it pictures Jesus as saying: 'Look around you, and see how the fields are ripe for harvesting' (John 4:35).

In this way the agricultural imagery that fed into Jesus' parables of growth and life became a daring, even terrifying challenge. God's kingdom has gifted us with life and growth. That gift becomes in turn our responsibility.

A PRAYER

O God, whose kingdom is growing powerfully in our
    midst,
let us marvel at that life which flourishes among us.
In your Son we receive life abundantly and forever.
Make us share his firm assurance
that at the end all things shall be well and wonderfully
    well.

EXERCISES

1 Where do you see the growth of God's kingdom happening?
2 Have there been any tiny beginnings in your life that have brought startling and fruitful conclusions?
3 Do you think most, if not all, of Jesus' parables describe his own life, work and destiny?
4 Draw a picture of Jesus as the tree of life.

---

1 We could make the same point in terms of light and truth. After 'en-lightening' us through his parables, Jesus came to be acknowledged as the Light of the world. Jesus spoke the truth, and was recognized as the (divine) Truth in person.

CHAPTER FIVE

THE LOST COIN
AND THE HIDDEN YEAST

Or what woman having ten silver coins, if she loses one of them, does not light a lamp, sweep the house, and search carefully until she finds it? When she has found it, she calls together her friends and neighbours, saying, 'Rejoice with me, for I have found the coin that I had lost.' Just so, I tell you, there is joy in the presence of the angels of God over one sinner who repents.

(Luke 15:8–10)

The kingdom of heaven is like yeast that a woman took and mixed in with three measures of flour until all of it was leavened.

(Matthew 13:33)

For some people, Christmas can act as an irritating reminder that we know so little about the life of Jesus – except for some crowded months at the end. Once his public ministry begins, we see him delivering his unique message, healing the sick, pardoning sinners and – as the opposition gathers with stunning speed – quickly becoming a man on the run. Action fills that last year or two. But before then Jesus lives through three decades about which we know next to nothing. We may be haunted by our incredibly slight information about his birth, childhood, youth and early manhood.

Some Christians coped with their bewilderment by giving their fantasies free rein and inventing answers to all the questions we or others might like to ask. The so called apocryphal gospels did their best to fill in the details about all those blanks in Jesus' life.

When the Holy Family arrived in Egypt, one account informs us, the temple idols crashed to pieces in front of the baby Jesus and the Pharaoh himself recognized him as truly divine. The apocryphal gospels chatter on also about the silent years in Nazareth. Some of these stories may seem mere pious imaginings, but others can be downright nasty. One story portrays Jesus walking through a village only to have another child bump into him. Jesus curses him and the child dies on the spot. The people of the village complain to Joseph, telling him to leave at once as their children are in danger. When Joseph passes on the complaint to Jesus, the villagers who complained are struck blind. Joseph sees what has happened, seizes Jesus' ear and gives it a good tug. The last point in the story may seem amusing. But the whole narrative exudes a taste for spiteful and murderous magic. Here, as elsewhere, we can appreciate that the Christian Church did well in refusing to accept such apocryphal gospels into the authoritative list of New Testament books.

But are we simply left then to put up with our very limited knowledge about so much of Jesus' life? Not altogether. Some conclusions can be legitimately drawn from the Gospels – in particular, from Matthew, Mark and Luke. There his preaching offers some clues as to the way in which his imagination formed during the years in Nazareth and worked to create his parables. The imagery and parables used by Jesus to guide us hint at the way he himself first perceived the world. But before exploring this line, let me insert three disclaimers.

THREE DISCLAIMERS

Here, as well as later and earlier in this book, I am not claiming that the Gospel writers give us an exact transcript of the words Jesus used. But I agree with many scholars that Matthew, Mark and Luke present a substantially accurate version of what Jesus said. As in what I have already written, in what follows I want to appeal only to those passages which seem to come from his preaching – in their general drift, if not necessarily in their precise wording. A pattern of images can come through, even where verbal expression may fluctuate and change somewhat.

Let me also add that Jesus obviously used some expressive language which others had provided. He inherited a rich and diverse storehouse of imagery which he could adopt and creatively employ in his preaching in general and in his parables in particular. An example is the world-tree from the Book of Daniel which we looked at in the last chapter and which seems to have played a part in shaping Jesus' parable of the sheltering mustard tree. Such imagery drawn from the past appeared to liberate – not block – his originality and to serve his special style of preaching. Nevertheless, I am not trying here to assess his degree of originality. The question is not: How uniquely inventive did Jesus show himself in his language? Rather, my question is: What does the imagery used by him suggest about the way he took in the world and saw things?

Let me add a third disclaimer for readers who may be nervous about orthodox Christian faith in Jesus' identity as Son of God. That's not being called into question. All the same, no appeal to his being the Word of God become flesh will tell us anything significant and detailed about the actual ways in which his human imagination operated. We may get some clues about that from the parables and other images in the Gospels.

After making these necessary presuppositions, let us come back to the case being developed in this chapter and, more broadly, in this book. The preaching of Jesus lets us glimpse the flow and flavour of his imagination which took shape during the hidden life at Nazareth. Let me pick out two features of his imagery, before focusing on two parables which reveal his attention to women.

TWO FEATURES OF JESUS' IMAGINATION

First, Jesus shows himself aware of and responsive to a broad range of human activity, suffering and happiness. He knows how farmers fatten calves for a feast, and knows that bumper harvests may call for extra barns. Although he offers no suggestions about thistle-control and the removal of rocks, he has observed that poor terrain can reduce the results of seeding. He recalls how people arrange parties, organize ceremonies and behave themselves at feasts. He has watched men and women putting patches on torn cloaks and using fresh wineskins for new wine. Jesus knows, too, popular ways for forecasting the weather: 'When you see a cloud rising in the west, you immediately say, "It is going to rain"; and so it happens. And when you see the south wind blowing, you say, "There will be scorching heat"; and it happens' (Luke 12:55–6).

Jesus does not flinch from facing human suffering. One of his memorable stories, which we will look at later, features a traveller who is robbed, beaten up and left half-dead on a country roadside. Jesus points to the greed of rich men which allows them to over-indulge, even though sick beggars lie starving in the streets outside. Human happiness does not pass Jesus by: the joy of a father whose renegade son returns, the celebrations at weddings, and – as we will see later – the delight of a housewife to have recovered some missing money.

When we put all his pictures together, we will see how Jesus speaks of a wide range of human activity: the role of stewards in large households, the administration of the law, the price of sparrows at the market, the right recipe for mixing yeast with flour, good and bad building practices, financial investments, and much else besides. Jesus' language in general and his parables in particular suggest an eye and an imagination that have scanned a good deal of normal human living. If we gathered together all his images, we would have a reasonably detailed sketch of daily life in ancient Galilee.

For the most part, Jesus' language reveals an imagination that has grown to be sensitively aware of what is going on in his world. Nevertheless, there are some gaps in the picture. And this is my second point about his imagery. He delights in children, but he has next to nothing to say about the mother–child relationship. Occasionally he glances at the father–child relationship: 'Is there any father among you who, if your child asks for a fish, will give a snake instead of a fish? Or if his child asks for an egg, will give a scorpion?' (Luke 11:11–12). But Jesus somehow finds his way around the mother–child relationship almost without pausing to notice it. When his eye runs forward to the troubles to come, he grieves over the sufferings that will afflict pregnant women and nursing mothers: 'Woe to the women who are pregnant and to those who are nursing infants in those days!' (Mark 13:17). Except for one or two such remarks, Jesus bypasses the mother–child relationship. Did he have such an utterly wonderful and (despite what we might draw from Luke 2:41–51) untroubled relationship to his own mother that this intimate area of life produced nothing for his language? Does it take the 'grit' of some tension in such areas to produce imaginative pearls? Whatever the reason, his preaching does not derive imagery from the mother–child relationship.

Almost as remarkable is his silence about the husband–wife relationship. He defends married life by rejecting divorce and insisting that even in their own minds men should not go lusting after other men's wives. He speaks of marriage feasts, wedding guests and the maidens who wait for the bridegroom to fetch his bride from her parents' home to his own. But there the imagery and the parables stop. Nothing survives from the preaching of Jesus about the loving and caring life together of married people, still less of marital tensions created by the couple themselves or coming from their children.

To illustrate the nature of prayer, Jesus tells a story about some tired and hungry traveller turning up at an ungodly hour and our needing to bother a neighbour even at midnight to borrow some food:

Suppose one of you has a friend, and you go to him at midnight and say to him, 'Friend, lend me three loaves of bread; for a friend of mine has arrived, and I have nothing to set before him.' And he answers from within, 'Do not bother me; the door has already been locked, and my children are with me in bed; I cannot get up and give you anything.' I tell you, even though he will not get up and give him anything because he is his friend, at least because of his persistence he will get up and give him whatever he needs.

(Luke 11:5–8)

We might have expected the story to run: 'Do not bother me. The door is now shut, and my wife and children are with me in bed.' But Jesus has the man say: 'My children are with me in bed.' Are we meant to suppose that the man in the story is a widower? Or that his wife is away visiting some relatives in another village? Or even that his marriage has broken up and that his wife is living with someone else? Or is it simply that Jesus is so sensitive and delicate that he will not say: 'Do not bother me. The door is now shut and my wife is with me in bed'?

Jesus differs from the Jewish scriptures he has prayerfully heard and read by not drawing images either from the mother–child or from the husband–wife relationships. Isaiah, the psalms and other Old Testament books made childbirth a common simile. To describe how the people were in agony and helpless without God, Isaiah says: 'Like a woman with child, who writhes and cries out in her pangs when she is near her time, so were we because of you, O Lord' (Isaiah 26:17). The tradition of such imagery moves with natural ease to depict Jerusalem being consoled by God in terms of nursing mothers and growing babies: 'Rejoice with Jerusalem, and be glad for her, all you who love her; rejoice with her in joy, all you who mourn over her – that you may suck and be satisfied from her consoling breast; that you may drink deeply with delight from her glorious bosom.' God goes on at once to promise: 'As a mother comforts her child, so I will comfort you' (Isaiah 66:10–13).

The husband–wife relationship likewise turns up frequently among Old Testament images. The sacred writers see positive possibilities in this relationship. Hosea celebrates God as the tender lover who longs to woo again his people and enjoy with them a kind of second honeymoon: 'I will now allure her, and bring her into the wilderness, and speak tenderly to her … she shall respond as in the days of her youth' (Hosea 2:14,15). But the Old Testament prophets also take up the husband–wife or man–woman relationship to focus the disobedience of God's people. To denounce the sins of the people, they repeatedly press into service ugly images of adultery and female prostitution. Ezekiel, in particular, develops horrible allegories of whores being lusted after and taken advantage of, only to be stripped, tortured and killed at the end (Ezekiel 16:1–63; 23:1–49). The prophets want to deliver a religious message: human sins grieve God just as a wife's infidelities grieve her loving husband. Their intention may be religiously serious but their language at times is gross.

Jesus himself never indulges in such language. He is always courteously delicate and never uses any demeaning language about women. Admittedly, such language is there in the scriptures that feed his prayer, but he never follows Ezekiel or any other prophet in coming out with anti-woman images. On the contrary, he lets us glimpse how he has seen God through what he knows of women and their activities.

With this we arrive at the fourth point which Jesus, our supreme spiritual director, would like us to appreciate about

God. In initiating us into the divine mystery, he has shown us that God is unconditionally loving (the parable of the prodigal son), utterly free (the parable of the labourers in the vineyard), and wonderfully powerful (the parables of growth and life). Now he encourages us to think that God can be seen to be like a woman doing ordinary things (such as baking bread) or coping with an emergency (such as a woman searching for lost property).

GOD AS A WOMAN

Unlike the parable of the mustard seed and some other parables, Jesus found nothing through prayerfully contemplating the scriptures that could give rise to his parables of the lost coin and the hidden yeast. Did he simply use his imagination to think up these two stories for himself? Or did he hear of a woman, perhaps one who lived nearby, who lost a tiny silver coin, found it after searching carefully, and then shared her joy with her friends and neighbours? Perhaps Jesus himself was one of those neighbours. It seems we are hearing from him a story that comes right out of his experience. Certainly in the case of the hidden yeast, from childhood on he had innumerable chances of seeing his mother and other women doing just what he says: mixing the right amount of yeast in the flour they were kneading for the oven. When he saw women doing that kitchen chore, his mind moved ever so easily to God. Years later in his preaching he wanted to share with us his experience, and invite us to let prayer arise for us from these and similar experiences.

The opening chapter of this book reflected on the story of the prodigal son, someone who is lost morally and religiously but is still able to make his own way home. The lost sheep with which Chapter 15 of Luke begins the three parables about loss has little chance of finding its way back through the wilderness to the shepherd and the rest of the sheep. Yet it could happen; a frightened and dim-witted sheep just might stumble on the right path. But a coin lost in a dusty corner of a badly lit house can't do anything itself to be found again. It pictures perfectly the helplessness of lost human beings who must wait to be found again. But they will be found; God will seek them out with the diligence and concern of a woman who has lost something valuable.

In his childhood Jesus watched his mother at work and saw for himself the power of a little yeast to affect a whole lump of dough. What comes from adding the yeast follows with certainty: the flour will rise, and a large, fragrant loaf will appear on the table. That elementary domestic experience entered the way Jesus thought about the growth of God's kingdom. The divine power may be hidden but it will certainly leaven everything. Immense and wonderful results are sure to come; we will eat bread together in the future kingdom of God.

Familiar, everyday experiences of the women around him entered Jesus' prayer and preaching. We would all do well to learn this lesson from his parables of the hidden yeast and the lost coin.

A PRAYER

> O Jesus, your preaching and parables show how sensitive you were to everyone and everything around you.
> Open our eyes to our world and to all the men and women who fill it.
> Share with us your sensitivity and respect for women, and let us see God shining through their lives and work.

EXERCISES

1 Compose a parable for yourself which begins 'the kingdom of heaven is like a woman who ...'
2 List all the attractive womanly images that you find in Isaiah 40–66.

3 What appeals to you about Jesus' relationships with women during his ministry?

4 What comments would you make on the following passage from Dorothy Sayers?

'Perhaps it is no wonder that the women were first at the cradle and last at the cross. They had never known a man like this man – there never has been such another. A prophet and teacher who never nagged at them, never flattered them, never treated them either as "The women, God help us!" or "The ladies, God bless them!"; who rebuked without querulousness and praised without condescension; who took their questions and arguments seriously; who never mapped out their sphere for them, never urged them to be feminine or jeered at them for being female; who had no axe to grind and no uneasy male dignity to defend; who took them as he found them and was completely unselfconscious. There is no act, no sermon, no parable in the whole Gospel that borrows its pungency from female perversity; nobody could possibly guess from the words and deeds of Jesus that there was anything "funny" about woman's nature.'

('Are Women Human?', *Unpopular Opinions*, London: Victor Gollancz, 1946, p. 119).

PART TWO

RECEIVING THE KINGDOM

CHAPTER SIX

THE TREASURE IN A FIELD
AND THE PEARL OF GREAT VALUE

The kingdom of heaven is like treasure hidden in a field, which someone found and hid; then in his joy he goes and sells all that he has and buys that field.

Again the kingdom of heaven is like a merchant in search of fine pearls; on finding one pearl of great value, he went and sold all that he had and bought it.

(Matthew 13:44–6)

All the parables in the Gospels give us a window on the mind and heart of Jesus. Nothing could be more marvellous and life-giving than to let these stories take us into his mind and heart. Even the shortest of them, parables of only one or two verses each, like those chosen for this chapter, can do that for us.

Thus far the parables which we have looked at highlight God's attitudes and activities. They give us Jesus' answers to the questions: What is God like? And what is God doing for us? Let us turn now to a series of parables in which Jesus opens up a vision of how human beings should respond to God's offer. The divine kingdom has gone on the market. What should be our reaction to this offer?

THE TREASURE IN A FIELD

The treasure hidden in a field evokes a gamut of feelings and insights. Despite warnings from some 'rigid' scholars that a parable makes only one point, those who prayerfully mull over this story which is only one verse in length will feel its rich range of meaning.

First, the parable speaks of the immeasurable value of something which comes as pure gift, not something the finder (perhaps a poor labourer) had ever worked for and expected. The divine kingdom has an incalculable worth like some magnificent treasure buried years before out in a field, perhaps when an invading army threatened to overrun the land and plunder everything within sight. The treasure God offers is colossal, and yet totally free and not needing to be earned.

Second, suddenly blundering on the treasure changes the whole world for the fortunate finder. This totally unexpected stroke of good fortune turns life around for the finder and fills him with ecstatic joy. All things have been made new for the lucky man.

Third, the finder must sacrifice everything if he is going to gain the treasure. He needs to 'sell all that he has', if he wants to buy the field which hides the immensely valuable prize that he has stumbled on. The treasure is there for the having, and the field is apparently up for sale.[1] But first the lucky finder must convert into cash the small amount of property he currently owns. He needs to sell everything, if he is going to secure everything and more than everything.

Fourth, it goes without saying that the chance of gaining such a treasure turns up only once in a lifetime, if even that. Finding a hidden hoard of gold gives us a chance that may never come again. Those who find such caches must instantly take advantage of their opportunity. They have to trust their quick judgement that the treasure is worth gaining at any cost and by any means. Immediately risking all and giving up all will make it possible to enjoy something that is truly a unique godsend.

As much as in any of his parables, Jesus brings out here how the kingdom is something that comes to us from God and yet it is also an adventure that we must venture on. The kingdom is an incredible 'godsend', something that is totally, completely and entirely God's work. And, at the same time, we should also realize that it is our affair, the good thing that turns up on our road through life and for which we must be ready to give up all – here and now.

Looking back at my own journey, I can name two or three occasions when, on the spur of the moment and with God's help, I took decisions that breathed fresh life into my existence. One came in 1964. I opened a letter in Germany from my religious superior in Australia; he asked me to prepare myself to teach foundational theology (an area of theology that deals with such basic themes as revelation, faith and the interpretation of the scriptures) and suggested doing a doctorate in Rome. I hadn't foreseen the letter, still less my own abrupt reaction. 'Writing a thesis in that branch of theology sounds like a good idea,' I thought. But at once I asked myself: 'But why don't I propose going to the University of Cambridge for that?' That snap decision enriched my life personally and academically for good. Hence I feel very much in tune with the man – was he a farm worker? – in Jesus' parable who unexpectedly comes across a wonderful treasure trove and instantly decides to profit from his discovery.

The Gospels themselves offer lovely examples that match the story of the treasure in the field: for instance, in the calling of two sets of brothers, Simon Peter and Andrew, and James and John:

As Jesus passed along the Sea of Galilee, he saw Simon and his brother Andrew casting a net into the sea – for they were fishermen. And Jesus said to them, 'Follow me and I will make you

fish for people.' And immediately they left their nets and
followed him. As he went a little farther, he saw James son of
Zebedee and his brother John, who were in their boat mending
the nets. Immediately he called them; and they left their father
Zebedee in the boat with the hired men, and followed him.

(Mark 1:16–18)

The two sets of brothers give us a wonderful instance of what
the parable of the treasure in the field can mean to individuals.
They have come across someone of immeasurable, incalculable
worth, Jesus himself. Suddenly, Peter, Andrew, James and John
are offered a magnificent treasure. It's totally free; they don't
have to work for it. Like the man who comes across the hidden
treasure, the two sets of brothers run into something, or rather
someone, who changes their whole world for them. Of course,
they have to give up something if they are going to gain the
treasure. The man in the parable sells everything he has to buy
the field and win the treasure. Peter, Andrew, James and John
must leave behind their boats, their fishing nets and their families if they are going to gain the colossal treasure, which is Jesus
himself. Finding a treasure like that is a 'godsend' that turns up
once in a lifetime, if that. Coming across the hidden hoard of
gold gives the man in the parable a chance that may never come
again. He has to trust his quick judgement: he must take advantage at once of his opportunity. Jesus is the incredible 'godsend'
for Peter, Andrew, James and John; a chance has turned up
and may never come again. They must trust their judgement
and risk all to follow Jesus. He is worth gaining at any cost, and
will bring them wonderful, lasting joy.

Those who come across the treasure will remember the
time and place for the rest of their lives. At the birth of
Christianity two sets of brothers found their treasure by the
Sea of Galilee. Many centuries later Paul Claudel, a French
writer and diplomat, praised the moment during the singing of
the office in the Cathedral of Notre Dame in Paris when his

heart was touched and he believed. It was Christmas Day 1886, and in the crowded congregation he was standing near the second pillar, at the entrance to the choir, on the right, and at the side of the sacristy. It was a moment of light and conversion that Claudel located very precisely and remembered for ever. He came across the treasure at that time and in that place. No one could forget such a moment of discovery.

THE PEARL OF GREAT VALUE

Jesus appears to have thought up the story of the hidden treasure for himself. At best the Book of Proverbs might perhaps have provided him with a slight pointer, when it spoke of searching for wisdom 'as for hidden treasures' (Proverbs 2:4). But in Jesus' story the lucky finder seems to run across the hoard and not to have been out looking for what he might find. Here the finder differs from the merchant who travels in deliberate search of the fine pearls that came from the Red Sea and the Indian Ocean. One day he comes across the kind of pearl he has long dreamed about. Its magnificence convinces him instantly to seize the chance that may never come again and buy that gleaming pearl.

This second parable calls to mind various passages in wisdom literature, above all those which encourage the search for wisdom (for instance, Proverbs 2:1–4; Wisdom 7:1–8:21). Yet Jesus takes up this theme of search in his own way and does not merely borrow from the scriptures he has inherited. What we find there, among other things, are poetical descriptions of Solomon's desire to have wisdom as his bride (Wisdom 8:2,9,16). Solomon values her more than 'any priceless gem', not to mention an abundance of gold and silver (Wisdom 7:9; see Job 28:1–19). Yet the very image Jesus chooses for his brief parable about the travelling merchant is that of a 'priceless gem'. Dare we hazard a guess about his choice and the motives for the choice?

Could it be that he did not like the image of a man travelling around the world in search of the perfect bride? Despite its positive possibilities, this image might demean women and reduce them to the object of a male search. Or did Jesus' choice stem from another source? While being conscious of being the divine Wisdom come among us in person, he knew himself to be the bridegroom (Mark 2:19–20) and not Lady Wisdom as bride. Whatever the reason, Jesus preferred to use the image of a merchant searching for fine pearls and not that of some latter-day Solomon out and about inspecting the marriage-market.

This parable of the precious pearl and that of the treasure highlight both the priceless value of what someone comes across and the right reaction on the part of the finder. To possess the glittering object, a wise person would instantly surrender everything. Such a chance of a lifetime rules out any half measures and any delay.

PREACHING AND PRACTICE

In his preaching Jesus transposes the two parables into peremptory claims he makes on those who respond favourably to the call of the kingdom but are not yet inclined to take instant action:

To another Jesus said, 'Follow me.' But he said, 'Lord, first let me go and bury my father.' But Jesus said to him, 'Let the dead bury their own dead; but as for you, go and proclaim the kingdom of God.' Another said, 'I will follow you, Lord, but let me first say farewell to those at my home.' Jesus said to him, 'No one who puts his hand to the plough and looks back is fit for the kingdom of God'.

(Luke 9:59–62)

Obedience to the call and gift of the kingdom must take precedence over everything else. Jesus spells out here what finding the treasure and the precious pearl could entail. One must instantly decide to 'sell all that one has' and at once secure the amazing gift of the kingdom. Not even the most sacred family ties and duties can stand in the way. If the kingdom of God has an incalculable value, it costs those who accept it nothing less than everything.

The magnificent treasure may carry a most painful price-tag. It may involve not only leaving people behind but even finding oneself in distressing conflict with one's nearest and dearest:

Do not think that I have come to bring peace to the earth, I have not come to bring peace, but a sword. For I have come to set a man against his father, and a daughter against her mother, and a daughter-in-law against her mother-in-law; and one's enemies will be members of one's own household.

(Matthew 10:34–6)

In this passage the repeated 'I have come' makes it clear how Jesus himself is the kingdom in person. Deciding for or against God's kingdom means deciding for or against Jesus. He is the treasure hidden in the field and the beautiful pearl of great value. Jesus himself is immeasurably valuable, someone who can most joyfully turn our lives around, the One who is a unique 'godsend' from whom we will receive everything if we are ready to lose everything.

We rightly interpret these two parables in terms of the very person of Jesus, who can turn the whole world around for each of us. We may also see the parables as autobiographical, expressions of what Jesus himself has based his own life on. For him God's will and the task of bringing us the divine kingdom are the treasure in the field and the priceless pearl for which he gives everything. He has said farewell to those at home, and never looks back. He gives his all to the task of proclaiming the kingdom. He has found God's kingdom; he lives for it and makes it accessible to others. He sacrifices everything for this task; at the end it will bring him to a violent death, because he has given his heart to his utterly precious mission for us.

A PRAYER

> Almighty, ever-living God,
> whose love surpasses all that we ask and deserve,
> open up for us the treasures of your mercy.
> Make us ever on the watch
> to cherish with all our hearts
> the gifts of grace which come from you.

EXERCISES

1 Have there been moments in your life when you have been given a 'godsend', a marvellous chance from God?
2 Do you think that the providence of God arranges the time and the place when we come across 'the treasure'?
3 Do you know people whose conversion stories exemplify the two parables examined in this chapter?

---

1 Recently two lawyers informed me that in certain countries today someone who concealed his find and bought the property from a freeholder could be sued later for not having declared his discovery. The law in the Middle East of Jesus' time did not seem to impose such obligations on fortunate finders. Nevertheless, while not legally obliged to report his discovery, the treasure-finder knew that he had to buy the field, if he were to keep the treasure without being challenged.

THE DISHONEST MANAGER

There was a rich man who had a manager, and charges were brought to him that this man was squandering his property. So he summoned him and said to him, 'What is this I hear about you? Give me an accounting of your management, because you cannot be my manager any longer.' Then the manager said to himself, 'What will I do, now that my master is taking the position away from me? I am not strong enough to dig, and I am ashamed to beg. I have decided what to do so that, when I am dismissed as manager, people may welcome me into their homes.' So, summoning his master's debtors one by one, he asked the first, 'How much do you owe my master?' He answered, 'A hundred jars of olive oil.' He said to him, 'Take your bill, sit down quickly, and make it fifty.' Then he asked another, 'And how much do you owe?' He replied, 'A hundred containers of wheat.' He said to him, 'Take your bill and make it eighty.' And his master commended the dishonest manager because he had acted shrewdly; for the children of this age are more shrewd in dealing with their own generation than are the children of light. And I tell you, make friends for yourselves by means of dishonest wealth so that when it is gone, they may welcome you into the eternal homes.

(Luke 16:1–9)

How should we deal with a critical situation, especially when time is running short? Through Jesus and his presence, our

God extends to us a graced time and a special chance. But we need to get moving quickly; the divine bargains will last for only a limited season. Hence Jesus introduces parables of crisis to fill out his teaching on our wise and rapid reaction to the coming of the kingdom.

Very likely Jesus had heard a number of stories about managers running big estates in the Galilean countryside for absentee landlords. From them he fashioned a parable about a superbly clever rascal who seizes his opportunity before time runs out on him. Faced with a dramatic crisis in his life, the crooked manager knows how to deal with it quickly. The slyness of such a deceptive person can teach everyone how to behave in a world plunged into an emergency as God comes on the scene with power. One must decide in favour of Jesus' message; any moment may be too late.

To illuminate this crisis of our times, Jesus doesn't limit himself to good characters like the father of the prodigal son, or to neutral figures like the merchant travelling in search of precious pearls. The behaviour of smart crooks, who feather their own nests or at least ensure themselves a happy future, can serve to challenge those faced with God's final offer to us. Even dishonest managers may have a lesson for those who let themselves learn from Jesus' parables.

Mismanagement and wasteful practices create a desperate crisis for a rich man's manager. Has he been using funds from the estate to hold lavish parties and live it up? Or perhaps the hostile charges brought against the manager are untrue and no more than false smears coming from the locals. Either way the owner is convinced that mismanagement, if not worse, has been taking place, and decides to dismiss his manager. Whatever the truth of the accusations and no matter what the manager produces in his final accounts, in a short time it is certain that he will become redundant. Apparently he has no savings to fall back on. Physically he is not strong enough to take work as a labourer. Psychologically he can't face cadging off people; he is too proud to beg. But, as the old saying has it, when the going gets tough, the tough get going. The manager, who so far has been guilty only of squandering the owner's property, now comes up with a dishonest scheme which will retrieve the situation and secure him a comfortable future after he loses his job.

Reading the story today we may jump to the conclusion: the manager was encouraging straight theft and covering his tracks by having his master's debtors change the contracts in their own handwriting, not his. But we need to remember the legal system of Jesus' time to have a more accurate view of what was going on. When making the contracts for the olive oil and wheat on behalf of the rich landowner, the manager would add an extortionate rate of interest and put everything down in one lump sum. Thus one debtor in the story had received only 450 gallons of olive oil. But, with interest being charged at 100 per cent, 100 jars or the equivalent of 900 gallons were written on the contract. The manager's job was to make as much money as possible for his master; the extra 50 jars of oil went to the landowner and did not finish up as commission in a manager's pocket. Apparently the interest on wheat was lower: only 20 per cent. The cunning manager had the second debtor eliminate that interest as well, by cancelling what would be today around 220 bushels of wheat. In both cases the manager told the debtors to strike out the interest that should have been paid to the rich landowner.

The picture then is this. The manager settles his grudge against his accusers and his boss by eliminating any profit for the landlord who is about to sack him. At the same time, the debtors will be more than happy at the cancelling of the interest. They are sure to repay the helpful manager by their hospitality and support. They will 'welcome him into their homes'. He has proved himself a 'friend' when he summons the debtors. In their turn they are sure to receive him when he loses his job.

The rich landlord, perhaps as much a rogue as the conman manager, somehow comes to hear about the interest being

eliminated. Amazingly, instead of punishing the rascal, he com-
mends him for having acted so shrewdly when caught in an
emergency. It's an astounding conclusion to Jesus' story.

In prayerfully reading through the story we must not miss
the soliloquy which Jesus sets at the heart of it all. When the
manager walks away from the interview knowing that he is to
be dismissed from his job, he doesn't indulge in self-pity and
start complaining to others that he's been wrongfully treated.
Instead he talks to himself and quickly assesses the situation
and his future prospects. At once he thinks of a way ahead and
acts decisively. He moves rapidly from asking himself 'What
will I do?' to a firm decision: 'I know what I shall do.' By introducing this brief soliloquy, Jesus invites us to identify with the
manager caught in a critical predicament and to think things
through quickly.

In effect, Jesus says to us:

**Don't dilly dally and waver. You hear my message of God's
kingdom. Time is running out on you. Respond to my message
quickly and shrewdly. Can't you let the smart decision of the
dishonest manager inspire you? Why don't you learn from him
and show just a little heavenly wisdom? The stakes are much
higher for you than for him. He secured hospitality for some
years or maybe the rest of his life – in the homes of his ex-
master's debtors. You are facing a decision that will determine
your eternal home.**

Jesus is appealing to us to show some enlightened common
sense, and to do so instantly.

It may well be that the parable as it originally came from
Jesus ended with the startling sentence: 'His master commended
the dishonest manager because he had acted shrewdly.' Drawing
on something Jesus may have said in another setting, the Gospel
of Luke adds: 'The children of this age are more shrewd in dealing with their own generation than are the children of light.

And I tell you, make friends for yourselves by means of dishonest wealth so that when it is gone, they may welcome you into the eternal homes.' This addition puts before us the further question: How best should we use material possessions to ensure our future security when this life is over? If we plan to trust in wealth as the earthly wisdom of this world would encourage us to do, we should remember: we can't take it with us. We should be shrewd in the way we use and divest ourselves of our own possessions, just as the dishonest manager showed himself shrewd in dealing with possessions that were not his own. We can convert our wealth into heavenly capital by sharing it now with those in great need.

ON SETTLING OUT OF COURT

The case of the dishonest manager presses the need to decide quickly and wisely. Faced with Jesus and his message, we cannot take our time. This example comes from business administration and the running of large estates for absentee landlords. Jesus takes up another image when urging us to decide rapidly in favour of the good news. This one comes from the contemporary court procedures:

Come to terms quickly with your accuser while you are on the way to court with him; or your accuser may hand you over to the judge, and the judge to the guard, and you will be thrown into prison. Truly I tell you, you will never get out until you have paid the last penny.

(Matthew 5:25–6)

Jesus knows, perhaps even from the experience of relatives and friends, that it is wise to avoid appearing before a judge, especially if one knows that the accuser is bringing a just case before the court and can prove it. Jesus' advice is: 'Settle with him at once before you both appear before the judge; otherwise you

may well be jailed and have a very unpleasant time of it.' Both
then and now, a timely reconciliation with the other party is
very often the most prudent thing to do. History continues to
be full of examples of people who stubbornly refuse to settle
out of court and then have to suffer costly and painful consequences.

Once again Jesus draws on the society around him, this time
not telling a particular story about some specific, if unnamed,
individual but reflecting rather on what happens frequently
enough in the administration of justice. Someone who knows
that he is in the wrong refuses to settle at once with his opponent, tries to bluff his way through the court, and fails to get
away with it. Then he will have to put up with a very distressing
outcome. In its own wonderful way the coming of God's kingdom puts us up against it. We have little time to make up our
minds. We must come to terms at once with this astonishing
chance God gives us through Jesus.

A King Planning War

On another occasion Jesus drives home the need to decide quickly and wisely by appealing to decisions rulers normally make
when faced with a critical disadvantage in military operations:

**What king, going out to wage war against another king, will not
sit down first and consider whether he is able with ten thousand
to oppose one who comes against him with twenty thousand? If
he cannot, then, while the other is still far away, he sends a del-
egation and asks for terms of peace.**

(Luke 14:31–2)

If outnumbered two to one, no king or general will join battle
unless he enjoys some peculiar advantage like leading a division
of highly trained elite troops. The Old Testament may tell how
Gideon needed only three hundred soldiers to destroy the

Midianites (Judges 7:1–8:3). But the scriptures attribute this victory to special help from God. Jesus appeals to the usual military strategy of his world, where a notable lack of combat troops demands a quick plea for peace. Those who hear the preaching of the kingdom should likewise make their move right away, and accept God's rule and all it entails.

INDIVIDUALS IN CRISIS

John's Gospel does not report Jesus' parables, but it transposes them in very personal terms. In particular, this Gospel gives us memorable stories of individuals who suddenly find themselves faced with the chance of a lifetime and react admirably in this crisis situation. I think of the Samaritan woman in chapter 4 and the man born blind in chapter 9. These are cases which vividly personalize those who open themselves to the crucial offer of the kingdom, which *is* Jesus himself. He is nothing more or less than God's kingdom in person.

In the Book of Revelation the risen Christ declares: 'Listen! I am standing at the door, knocking; if you hear my voice and open the door, I will come in to you and eat with you, and you with me' (Revelation 3:20). This verse serves to sum up beautifully a special feature of John's Gospel: the momentous chance individual men and women suddenly have when Jesus encounters them. From the first to the last chapter we can read this Gospel in that key – as series of crucial one-to-one encounters with Jesus. To be sure, he also meets groups or even crowds of people. But much of the story concerns meetings with individuals. Sometimes these individuals bear names like Nicodemus and Mary Magdalene. Sometimes, like almost everyone in Jesus' parables, they are not identified by name.

Here I propose to reflect on encounters with two on the anonymous list from John: the Samaritan woman and the man born blind. Let me take these two stories in their own dramatic terms as John's Gospel presents them, and yet as they also

serve to illustrate how people might quickly come to terms with
and accept God's unique blessing held out to them in Jesus.
Some patterns will emerge when we put four questions to the
two cases we are taking up: How do these two individuals come
to meet Jesus? What might they expect from him? How are they
changed? How does the outcome go far beyond their initial
expectations?

The Samaritan Woman

It looks like an accident that the Samaritan woman meets Jesus
(John 4:4–42). She could have gone to draw water earlier or
later in the day. The midday encounter at Jacob's well seems
a perfectly chance meeting. But what begins like a random
exchange ends very differently.

Unlike some other stories in John's Gospel in which individuals seek Jesus out, here it is he himself who takes the initiative and opens the dialogue with the Samaritan: 'Give me a
drink.' To begin with, their interchange centres on something
which is not only simple and basic, but also an elemental necessity for human beings and their world – water. The first half of
the dialogue ends with Jesus' promise: 'Those who drink of the
water that I will give them will never be thirsty. The water that
I will give will become in them a spring of water gushing up to
eternal life.'

When I read that promise, I always think of the fountains
in the Villa d'Este outside Rome. The spouts of crystal-fresh
water leap into the air and become charged with sunlight.
Like those fountains, Jesus gives himself away with joy. The
Samaritan woman and the rest of us are not asked to search and
dig for water, let alone store it up in some reservoir. We simply
have to cup our hands and drink.

The encounter at high noon abruptly moves on when Jesus
says to the woman, 'Go, call your husband.' Jesus has touched
her irregular home situation. She has had five husbands, and
is now living with a man who is not her husband. But she does

not break off the dialogue with Jesus in embarrassment. Little by little she lets him lead her on, right to the point where he no longer speaks of living water but reveals himself as the living Christ.

At once we see the missionary impulse in a person who has experienced Jesus at depth. She does not hoard the news but brings it straightaway to the people of Sychar. Many are so impressed by the woman's testimony that they come to believe in Jesus. Later, others tell her that she is now superfluous: 'It is no longer because of what you said that we believe, for we have heard for ourselves, and we know that this is truly the Saviour of the world.' They no longer need the woman's witness to Jesus for themselves, and they call him by a title we find nowhere else in the New Testament: 'the Saviour of the world'.

The sinful Samaritan woman is no slow learner – quite the opposite. This might seem all the more surprising in someone who is no young teenager but a grown woman with a steady habit of getting married. In the encounter with Jesus she lets herself be touched, changed and loved by him. Within a few hours she has become a missionary for him.

It is the story of someone who gets up one morning suspecting and expecting nothing. The day ends with her a totally changed person. She lets Jesus encounter, challenge and reveal himself to her as God's kingdom in person.

A MAN BLIND FROM BIRTH

His disciples are with him when Jesus first meets the man who has been blind from birth (John 9:1–41). They see the poor chap sitting there and begging, but show themselves quite blind to his misery and also to the power of Jesus. They do not ask their master to intervene. Rather, they treat the blind man as a good occasion for a theological discussion: 'Rabbi, who sinned, this man or his parents, that he was born blind?'

The blind man himself does not say anything, let alone ask
for a cure. Somehow he already knows Jesus' name and presumably is heartened by what he hears Jesus say:

**Neither this man nor his parents sinned; he was born blind so
that God's works might be revealed in him. We must work the
works of him who sent me while it is day; night is coming when
no one can work. As long as I am in the world, I am the light of
the world.**

Then Jesus takes the initiative and anoints the blind man's eyes
with clay. Now the blind man has something to do. He must
go and wash his eyes in the pool of Siloam. He does that and
comes back seeing for the first time in his life.

At this point Jesus has left the stage, so to speak. In the
Fourth Gospel there is no other passage in which he remains so
long offstage (John 9:7b–34). But the man who now sees fills
the scene as he begins to speak and act with simple vigour. He
begins also to suffer in new ways.

Encountering Jesus means pain as well as healing. The man
born blind would have learned long ago to cope with his situation. Then Jesus comes along to heal him, but also to disturb
his relationship with his parents and bring him into conflict
with the religious authorities (John 9:13–34).

But the man born blind moves quickly from truth to truth.
He first recognizes 'the man called Jesus' as a 'prophet' and
'from God'. Finally, he worships Jesus and expresses his faith:
'Lord, I believe.' His encounter with Jesus has moved steadily
to that supreme moment.

What leads him there is his willingness to trust his experience and make up his own mind. The religious authorities badger him and in the name of God's sacred laws try to force him
to agree that Jesus is a sinner. After all, the healing work has
taken place on the sabbath. But the man born blind stands his
ground and insists on what he has experienced: 'I do not know

whether he is a sinner. One thing I do know, that though I was blind, now I see.' Further quick reflection on this experience makes him realize the startling nature of what has happened: 'Never since the world began has it been heard that anyone opened the eyes of a person born blind. If this man were not from God, he could do nothing.' When Jesus returns in search of him, the man born blind is ready to confess his faith.

The lessons Jesus teaches through the story of the dishonest manager and the advice to settle quickly out of court we find exemplified in the Samaritan woman and the man born blind. They react quickly and wisely to the coming into their lives of the kingdom, which is nothing more nor less than the coming into their lives of Jesus himself.

A PRAYER

> Lord, give me the grace to recognize what you offer me.
> Make me move quickly to embrace your rule and kingdom.
> Let me welcome into my life the supreme gift of your Son's presence.

EXERCISES

1 Have you ever known someone who reacted to the threat of dismissal with the shrewdness of the dishonest manager? Could you follow Jesus in finding that such dishonesty illuminates the right reaction to the challenge of God's kingdom?

2 How often in your life have you experienced God giving you some astonishing chance and grace? How did you react?

3 Do you think it possible for someone's life to be turned around in a single day, as we see in the cases of the Samaritan woman and the man born blind?

CHAPTER EIGHT

THE SOWER

Listen! A sower went out to sow. And as he sowed, some seed fell on the path, and the birds came and ate it up. Other seed fell on rocky ground, where it did not have much soil, and it sprang up quickly, since it had no depth of soil. And when the sun rose, it was scorched; and since it had no root, it withered away. Other seed fell among thorns, and the thorns grew up and choked it, and it yielded no grain. Other seed fell into good soil and brought forth grain, growing up and increasing and yielding thirty and sixty and a hundred-fold.

(Mark 4: 3–8)

Attentive reading of the Gospels shows us a remarkable 'hereness' and 'nowness' about Jesus' language. Images drawn from history, current world affairs and geography hardly surface in his preaching. He is not interested in the wider world of education, art and culture. His eye is caught by the scene right in front of him. He recalls, of course, a few episodes from biblical history and legend, like the story of the flood and the destruction of Sodom. But in general he betrays little interest in the past.

Jesus never mentions that founding event of Jewish history, the deliverance from slavery in Egypt. The Maccabean revolt, the Hasmonean period, the capture of Jerusalem by Pompey in

63 BC, the switch of Jewish allegiance to Julius Caesar, the reign of Herod the Great (37–4 BC) and all the other crowded events of recent history never even get a passing nod in Jesus' preaching That larger world of politics fails to come into sight. Apart from a brief remark about paying taxes to Caesar (Mark 12:13–17) and a comment on some victims of Pilate's brutality (Luke 13:1), Jesus hardly even suggests that he lives under indirect Roman rule.

Once, as we saw in the last chapter, Jesus draws a lesson from a military buildup – the king with only ten thousand troops deciding not to risk war against a king with twenty thousand troops (Luke 14:31–2). But Jesus names no specific king nor any particular cold-war situation in the Mediterranean world of the first century. Another time he speaks vaguely of a 'nobleman' who 'went to a distant country to get royal power for himself and then return' (Luke 19:12). But he mentions no historical figure as the peg on to which he hangs the parable of the pounds that follows. Jesus' mind reaches out to the immediate situation in the here and now. He neither scans history, not even the most recent history, nor lets his eye run around the Roman Empire for images and examples that he could press into service.

At times, the preaching of Ezekiel and other classic prophets takes us around the world of their day: Persia, Egypt, Cyprus, Tarshish, Greece, southern Russia, and a range of other places. But the known geography of his day provides little or no imagery for Jesus. His preaching never even suggests that he lives near the Mediterranean. He shows no interest in evoking other locales, still less in seeing more of the world for himself.

In short, there is an obvious hereness and nowness about the language of Jesus, a preoccupation with the scene right in front of him. He does not share in that romantic imagination which revels in ancient times and far-away places.

Along with this sense of the immediate situation, Jesus reveals a kind of earthy particularity in his language in general and parables in particular. Characteristically, he answers general questions like 'Who is my neighbour?' by telling a story (Luke 10:29–37). Of course, others have done that – both before and after Jesus. But the fact that they can also display this habit does not make it any less his own. He thinks from below, not by way of deduction from above. He offers cases from which his audience can draw general principles, if they want to. Even his more generalizing remarks stay close to the earth: 'No one after drinking old wine desires new wine' (Luke 5:39). There is a common touch in the proverbial sayings he cites: 'Doubtless you will quote to me this proverb, "Doctor, cure yourself!"' (Luke 4:23). He invites his hearers to take in and think through the things around them. His imagination is attuned to the wisdom of ordinary people. All of this makes him the supreme preacher with the common touch. He speaks with us and to us, not merely at us. He more than merits the modern title of Jesus the Communicator.

RECEIVING THE SEED

In one of his best-known parables Jesus talks of something that continues to happen constantly in different parts of the world: a farmer sowing his fields. Jesus takes up this very common activity, which some of his audience routinely engage in and all are familiar with. He might have taken this story in a different direction by talking about the impact of the weather which follows the seeding. A drought, a cloudburst or just the right amount of rainfall have always determined the size of the harvest. But instead of weaving in three variations in rainfall, Jesus pitches his parable in terms of the soil. The rainfall comes from heaven and, until very recently, has been more or less completely beyond human control. But the cultivation of the soil belongs very much in our domain – along with all the other things which we do (such as working in vineyards, mixing yeast in flour and 'adjusting' people's bills) and which Jesus introduces into his other stories.

The parable of the sower sets out first three different reasons why the seed may fail to produce the desired crop. The seed can fall on a path, on rocky ground or among thorns. The growth depends on where it finishes up and how it is received. Good soil will guarantee a fine yield of grain. But from the outset no one in their right mind will expect crops to flourish along paths, on rocky ground or among thorns.

Here we could feel like taking a cue from that satire in the Book of Judges where various trees speak and, finally, brambles have their say (Judges 9:7–15). In Jesus' parable, a path, a patch of rocky ground and a clump of thorns might speak up and say: 'If you're a path, rocky ground and a thornbush, how can you be expected to bring forth any effective growth? The sower has been a rather careless chap. Why doesn't he look where he's throwing the seed? It's his fault, not ours, if some seed gets eaten up, withers away or gets choked.'

Without engaging in special pleading for the farmer, I think we should remember that he is to be pictured as moving over an unploughed field. Jesus imagines someone sowing before he ploughs the field and thus turns the seed into the ground to wait for rain and growth. At the time of sowing it can easily happen that some soil lightly covers tracks across the field, patches of rocky ground, and clumps of thorns which have been cut down but not totally eradicated. Ploughing will expose the problems. But by then it will be too late. The farmer has already sowed his seed across the whole field.

What then is Jesus driving at in this parable? What light does it shed on the reception of the divine kingdom? To begin with, there will be severe problems: frustrated starts, failures, smothering opposition and trials galore. Yet, despite all the obstacles met in sowing the seed on various kinds of soil, the farmer's work will succeed. His sowing will bring a harvest, which Jesus also describes in a triple fashion: 'yielding thirty and sixty and a hundred-fold'. To emphasize the ultimate success that will follow Jesus' preaching of the kingdom, he gives an extraordinary twist to the size of the harvest. The yield will not simply be thirty- or sixty-fold, but something quite remarkable: even a hundred-fold. The kingdom of God will enjoy that kind of astounding success. In brief, the story of the sower portrays an astonishing contrast: between initial challenges and amazing success at the end.

Inevitably this parable implies the different ways in which human beings receive God's incredibly generous offer. Their reception will be either favourable or unfavourable. Despite the triple scheme of no soil, rocky soil and ground already occupied by thorns, in all three cases the good seed will yield nothing. There will be variations in the harvest from the good soil, but the seed will always bring a yield of at least thirty-fold. The parable presents us with a stark either/or. For one group, different forces may be at work to block the harvest, but in none of these cases can the seed have its proper effect. The other group, represented by the good soil, may vary in the size of the yield, yet all of them will bring in a fruitful yield.

The verbs that thread through the parable hint at an option between life and death. Some seed is eaten, scorched, withers away or is choked. Other seed grows up, increases, brings forth and yields a harvest. These verbs put the choice: be devoured or be productive.

This sharp alternative belongs as well to other parables which picture the reception of the kingdom. Either the man who finds the treasure hidden in the field will take the plunge and buy the field, or else he will miss out on the glorious treasure he has stumbled across. The merchant who finds the pearl of his dreams will either give everything to have it, or for the rest of his life he will regret his timidity. The dishonest manager will either act quickly to secure for himself a comfortable future, or will suffer from misery as a result of being dismissed from his well-paying job.

The parable of the sower brings in thus a sense of our responsibility when faced with the chance of entering God's final kingdom. We can happily succeed or culpably fail when given this grace of a lifetime. Yet here we may become a little puzzled if we recall a similar parable, that of the seed which grows silently right through to harvest (Mark 4:26–32).

As we saw in Chapter 4, it is God who gives life and growth. We don't know how, but the divine energy will bring overwhelming results. Is it possible to reconcile the different pictures which come from two parables, both to be found in the very same chapter of Mark's Gospel? Jesus offers us no theological solution – at least no speculative solution such as those coming from theologians who for centuries have wrestled over the apparent conflict between divine grace and human freewill. Rather, Jesus offers us two stories, which interact with and qualify each other. We might paraphrase what he preaches by saying: 'The coming of the kingdom is totally, completely and utterly God's work. At the same time, the coming of the kingdom is totally, completely and utterly the work of human beings.' Even so, this paraphrase does not match the vigorous earthiness and power of Jesus' two parables. One is always advised to mull over Jesus' stories rather than stick to any paraphrase.

A PRAYER

O loving Father, your kingdom grows in our world,
and will flourish astoundingly at the end.
Let us feed on your Son's teaching and presence,
so that our lives will yield the hundred-fold he
so desires.

EXERCISES

1 What do you like about the directness and common touch of Jesus' preaching? What Gospel passage exemplifies this best for you?

2 Imagine that the farmer's crop is destroyed by a plague of locusts, a plant disease or a brushfire. What would happen in those cases to Jesus' parable?

3 Is there any connection to be drawn between the grain that grows in abundance and Jesus himself as 'the bread of life' (John 6:25–58)?

CHAPTER NINE

THE TALENTS

The kingdom of heaven is as if a man, going on journey, summoned his servants and entrusted his property to them; to one he gave five talents, to another two, to another one, to each according to his ability. Then he went away. The one who had received the five talents went off at once and traded with them, and made five more talents. In the same way, the one who had the two talents made two more talents. But the one who had received the one talent went off and dug a hole in the ground and hid his master's money. After a long time the master of these servants came and settled accounts with them. Then the one who had received the five talents came forward, bringing five more talents, saying, 'Master, you handed over to me five talents; see, I have made five more talents.' His master said to him, 'Well done, good and trustworthy servant; you have been trustworthy in a few things, I will put you in charge of many things; enter into the joy of your master.' And the one with the two talents also came forward, saying, 'Master, you handed over to me two talents; see, I have made two more talents.' The master said to him, 'Well done, good and trustworthy servant; you have been trustworthy in a few things, I will put you in charge of many things; enter into the joy of your master.'

Then the one who had received the one talent also came forward, saying, 'Master, I knew that you were a harsh man, reaping where you did not sow, and gathering where you did not scatter seed; so I was afraid, and I went and hid your talent in the ground. Here you have what is yours.' But the master replied, 'You wicked and lazy servant! You knew, did you, that

I reap where I did not sow, and gather where I did not scatter? Then you ought to have invested my money with the bankers, and on my return I would have received what was my own with interest. So take the talent from him, and give it to the one with ten talents. For to all those who have, more will be given, and they will have an abundance; but from those who have nothing, even what they have will be taken away. As for this worthless servant, throw him into the outer darkness, where there will be weeping and gnashing of teeth.'

(Matthew 25:14–30)

CHRISTIANITY FOR LOSERS?

One of the saddest comments you can hear passed on somebody is that he is a born loser. When we hear someone described as a born loser, we know roughly speaking what is meant. The person in question seems to have an innate knack of making things go badly. Or at least things always appear to go badly for him.

Sometimes it can look as if hearing the message of the kingdom and following Jesus means joining the ranks of the born losers. That is what an Australian friend of mine suggested to me once when he turned away from his television set and remarked: 'Christianity is for losers; success is for tennis players.' He had just been watching some Australian champion win a Grand Slam tournament; at the time he himself was feeling pretty depressed about his own life and faith. Was my friend right? Is being captivated by Jesus and following him really for losers? For that matter, is Jesus himself a born loser?

The parable of the talents appears to suggest the exact opposite. It seems to imply that Christianity is for winners. Success is for the competent disciples. The story from Matthew's Gospel maximizes the importance of expertise and accomplishments. Those who receive their master's funds and invest them successfully are highly praised and rewarded. They refuse to play for safety, and boldly prove themselves superb investors. Both of them double the money given them, and make 100 per cent profit. They are the ones who hear the promise 'I will put you in charge of many things', and the invitation 'enter into the joy of your master'. Apparently God's arithmetic favours winners: 5 + 5 = 10; 2 + 2 = 4; but 1 + 0 = 0.

This may seem like the right reading of Jesus' parable. Successful performance will be rewarded; salvation is measured by work; Christian discipleship is for winners. The winners take all.

The section of Matthew's Gospel which immediately precedes our passage tells the story of ten bridesmaids (Matthew 25:1–13). The five prudent ones become the winners in the group of ten. In its implications this is a somewhat less cheerful story than the parable of the talents, which presents two out of three servants as successful. Only 50 per cent of the bridesmaids, instead of 66 per cent of the servants, turn out winners. But the point remains, apparently, the same. The accent is on performance – prudent performance by the five bridesmaids, successful performance by the two servants.

A CRITICAL TASK

But let us take a closer look at the story of the talents. As we will see happens in the story of the good Samaritan, Jesus puts three characters right up front in his parable of the talents: three servants or staff-members of a big estate, who each receive extraordinary amounts of money. Story-tellers of a later age might have spoken of an Englishman, an Irishman and a Scotsman being entrusted, respectively, with five bags of gold, two bags of gold and one bag of gold. However we care to put it, Jesus is talking about three persons who receive very large amounts of money. In today's terms, even the servant who receives only one talent is given the equivalent of more than fifteen years' wages for a labourer. This would be over £200,000 in the United Kingdom and well over $300,000 in the USA.

The other two receive over £1,000,000 and over £400,000, respectively. When the rich businessman later speaks of their being 'trustworthy in a *few* things', he is indulging a big understatement.

The wealthy owner is leaving on a journey abroad. We are not told where he is going, how far away he will be or what he plans to do. He simply leaves home and will be gone a long time. The scenario differs obviously from that of the prodigal son. He goes to a distant country, dissipates his fortune, will return home after being away for some time, perhaps only a matter of months rather than years.

Before the owner takes off, we do not hear about any family arrangements he has to make. Is he married and with children? Does he have sons, like the father of the two boys in Luke 15? If he does, are these still too young to be left in charge of the property? Are there any aged and infirm parents to be taken care of?

And, for that matter, where does all the money come from? Did the wealthy owner inherit it, or did he gain it all through hard work and skilful investments? The story seems to hint that the man ran his business in an immoral way. Some scholars take the words about 'reaping where he does not sow and gathering where he does not scatter' to imply he was not only a high-risk speculator but also exploited others. He demands excessively high rates of interest for any loans. But Jesus doesn't want us to be distracted by such questions, let alone by any answers to them. He tells a spare, economic story which concentrates on the owner and three of his servants.

The rich man recognizes that his three servants differ in ability and assigns various sums to each of them. Yet even the third, who receives only one talent, receives a very considerable amount. The owner entrusts a great deal to them, obviously expecting the three of them to do something with those funds. Unlike the labourers in the vineyard, none of them are given specific instructions, let alone a specific task to do. Everything is left to their initiative.

The master is then absent 'for a long time'. Here the parable of the talents reflects nothing of the kind of vital urgency which we find in such parables as those of the treasure in the field, the merchant who finds a precious pearl, and the dishonest manager. In those three stories, action must be taken at once. The offer of the kingdom brings the sudden chance of a lifetime; we must decide now, for any moment may be too late. This pressure of time does not come through the parable of the talents. But the utter seriousness of our situation does. Sooner or later, the day of reckoning will arrive.

The kingdom of God presents us with a critical task. In this interim, indefinite period as we wait for the end, we cannot afford to be timid or slothful. Jesus wants us to make the most of the graces and chances we have been given. He longs to be able to say to each of us, 'come into the home of your loving Father and enjoy life with us for ever'. In the meantime, however, the kingdom of God gives each of us a crucial task to perform.

It is the critical nature of our task that explains the difference between the three servants and the different way they are treated at the end. The first two servants are not afraid to bring the gold given them out into the open, to take it to the marketplace, and to let it go in investments. They may have indulged in illegal business practices like their employer. At all events, they increase his capital one hundredfold. The third servant, however, is afraid to bring the money out into the open and do business with what has been entrusted to him. He takes careful precautions against theft or loss by secretly hiding the gold in the ground. The first two servants show no fear, or at least they ignore any nervous worry about letting the money go when trading with it. The third servant is afraid of losing his one talent. He is terrified about letting the money slip out of his hands, and scared of any risks. He does not even put the money into a bank, probably because he fears it might go bankrupt. In short, the first two let go, while he holds on grimly and fearfully. He doesn't lose the money, but doesn't gain a penny either.

This way of reading the failure of the third servant comes from his own explanation, 'I was afraid.' However, the master's reply, 'you wicked and *lazy* servant', brushes aside any excuse based on fear, and suggests that sloth has been the problem. The servant has been too lazy and fearful even to go and invest the money with the bankers. That would have brought in at least some interest, even if he couldn't expect the kind of profit that bold trading might bring.

Whether he has given in to fear, sloth or both, readers can only wonder why the servant is treated so harshly. The owner seems surprisingly hard on him in having him kicked out into 'the outer darkness, where there will be weeping and gnashing of teeth'. What has the servant done that is so wicked? He hasn't stolen the talent; he has scrupulously guarded it so that he can return the whole sum intact. Why should he be dealt with so severely? To speak the language of a later time, he belongs to a firm that values risk-taking and high returns. He doesn't match that expectation and so loses everything he has. He is booted out, and enjoys no future in the world of fast finance.

This may also help to explain the reward for the other two servants, which could look excessively generous. Both of them are 'put in charge of many things', and invited into 'the joy' of their master; the first, who did so well when entrusted with five talents, is also awarded the remarkable bonus of a talent for himself.

The justification Jesus offers for what happens in rewarding the first two servants and punishing the third may well strike us as unfair: 'To all those who have, more will be given, and they will have in abundance; but from those who have nothing, even what they have will be taken away.' It all sounds like a grim either/or; no middle ground is allowed. The winners take all; the losers lose everything. The rich get richer, and the poor get poorer.

Clearly Jesus hopes that this story will bring home to us that the task we receive for the kingdom of God is a life and death matter. There is no middle ground. Jesus wants to convince us that we each face a crucial and critical task: one tailored to our personal abilities, but utterly crucial and critical just the same. No fear or sloth should be allowed to get in the road of carrying through the work we have been given. God acts most generously, and all is gift. We must use the divine gifts courageously and not capitulate to fear or immobility. We are given only one chance, literally the chance of a lifetime.

Some might be tempted to rewrite Jesus' parable and have the rich owner deal more gently with the third servant. He could, for instance, say: 'Look, you didn't perform successfully this time round. You should take a few tips from those other two servants, and then go out and try again. They should be able to tell you where it would be wise to invest the talent. I'll let you have another year or two for this second try.' The owner, and even more God, can seem unreasonable and terrifyingly demanding. But we can't say that we weren't warned. Jesus could hardly be clearer in bringing out what a life and death matter our one big chance for the kingdom really is.

ON NOT BEING AFRAID TO BE A LOSER

Let me go back to my friend. Was he right in thinking that Christianity is for losers and success is for tennis players? I thought about his remark for a long time, and finally decided that he missed out by just a fraction on the truth. But it's that fraction which looks vital. In the light of Jesus' parable of the talents, one must say that Christianity is for those who are not afraid to be losers, those who are not nervous about losing their gifts, those who are not afraid to let their talents come out into the open.

Jesus' message is for those who trust that boldly giving and courageously investing does not diminish but enhances. At some church services we hold a lighted candle in our hand and are asked to share the light with others. But our light is not thereby diminished. By giving light to others, we gain from their new brilliance.

Once again we will understand a parable from Jesus if we interpret it as autobiographical: implicitly he is also talking about himself, the Bold Investor for his heavenly Father. Jesus is not afraid to be a loser. He will let himself become like a grain of wheat falling into the ground. He will refuse to lose his nerve at the possibility of being swallowed up by failure. He never decides against investing everything for our sake because he fears that there will be no return. In brief, Jesus' own life, death and resurrection dramatize his parable of the talents. Who has ever received more, given more and won more than him? He shows himself to be *par excellence* the servant with five talents, and ever so much greater than him.

There is, then, a world of difference between being born losers and those who are not afraid to be losers. Jesus himself had no special knack of making things go badly, but he was not afraid if they seemed to go badly. He was not born to lose, but he was ready to accept that success might come only after defeat and apparent failure. Likewise, following Jesus is for those who are not afraid of being losers. It is the task for those who refuse to capitulate to nervousness about being swallowed up, about somehow missing out and finding themselves losing everything.

Jesus shares rich gifts with us. He wants success, success with all the graces and talents entrusted to us. He has given us his riches; he also wants to bring us into the joy of his heavenly home. His followers are men and women called to act boldly, put aside all sloth, invest fearlessly and trade with their lives without becoming timidly anxious about losing everything. In a word, Christianity is for those who are not afraid to be losers.

None of us has any other conscience to examine except our own when we ask: 'Am I ready to invest without fear of failure, to give without any terror over losing, to use my talents without any anxiety at being used up?' In framing our answer, we look steadily at Jesus, the fearless investor, the resurrected 'failure', and the one who never gave in to the fear of becoming a loser.

A PRAYER

> Give us, O God, the courage which comes only from you,
> that courage which will let us follow your Son fearlessly.
> Give us the energy to perform to the end the tasks you have given us.
> Thus may we all enter into the joy of your kingdom.

EXERCISE

Take some time to read the parable of the pounds in Luke 19:11–27. How does it resemble and differ from the parable of the talents? Which story do you prefer and why? Don't miss the way the nobleman of the parable of the pounds, before leaving for a distant country, entrusts a pound (at that time the equivalent of about three months' wages for a labourer) to each of his *ten* servants or slaves. But when the man returns (after how long a delay?) and now enjoys royal power, we hear only from *three* of his servants. The similarities and differences between the two parables suggest drawing up two parallel columns on a sheet of paper. One could then make at a glance a comparison and contrast.

PART THREE

LIVING THE KINGDOM

CHAPTER TEN

THE UNFORGIVING SERVANT

The kingdom of heaven may be compared to a king who wished to settle accounts with his servants. When he began the reckoning, one who owed him ten thousand talents was brought to him; and, as he could not pay, his lord ordered him to be sold, together with his wife and children and all his possessions, and payment to be made. So the servant fell on his knees before him, saying, 'Have patience with me, and I will pay you everything.' And out of pity for him, the lord of that servant released him and forgave him the debt. But that same servant, as he went out, came upon one of his fellow servants who owed him a hundred denarii, and seizing him by the throat, he said, 'Pay what you owe.' Then his fellow servant fell down and pleaded with him, 'Have patience with me, and I will pay you.' But he refused; then he went and threw him into prison until he would pay the debt. When his fellow servants saw what had happened, they were greatly distressed, and they went and reported to their lord all that had taken place. Then his lord summoned him and said to him, 'You wicked servant! I forgave you all that debt because you pleaded with me. Should you not have had mercy on your fellow servant, as I had mercy on you?' And in his anger the lord handed him over to be tortured until he would pay his entire debt. So my heavenly Father will also do to every one of you, if you do not forgive your brother or sister from your heart.

(Matthew 18:23–35)

With this parable we open the third part of this book, which asks the question: How does Jesus expect us to behave towards one another and towards God, once we have received the uniquely wonderful gift of the divine kingdom? Jesus' primary directive is nothing if not clear: 'Be merciful, just as your Father is merciful' (Luke 6:36). A command of this importance simply has to find its way into a parable. Hence Jesus gives us the remarkable story of the unforgiving debtor or merciless servant.

THE UNFORGIVING DEBTOR

The servant owes the king a mind-boggling sum: in current terms around £2,250,000,000, or over US$3,600,000,000. How has he managed to borrow so much or get so far into debt? Maybe he is the governor of a large province and the tax has not been paid for several years. Perhaps he has lost the money on projects which collapsed. We are not told; we are simply presented with an utterly desperate debt, one that simply couldn't be paid off even by selling into slavery the defaulting debtor along with his family and by liquidating all his property. The debt comes across as breathtaking; so too does the amazing act of generosity on the part of the king. He goes far beyond what the debtor asks. At his wits' ends, the servant falls on his knees and pleads despairingly for some more time, without specifying how much. 'Out of pity' the king turns around and cancels the whole debt – an act of unbelievable magnanimity.

If the parable were to stop at that point, we would be left with a striking picture of the divine mercy. We are impossibly indebted to God. But this does not make our situation hopeless. Our God shows amazing mercy towards us. The divine forgiveness goes far beyond anything we might imagine and even ask for.

However, the parable presses on relentlessly. The forgiven debtor leaves the court of the king and immediately runs into someone who owes him a relatively small amount: around

£6,000 or over US$9,000, maybe a loan made out of the huge sum owed to the king. This debt seems a trifle compared with the debt which the king has cancelled a few moments before. But the story goes ahead – not with a happy replay of what we have just read, but with a depressingly mean-minded outcome. The servant who has been forgiven the enormous debt now finds himself in the role of creditor, and he is asked for an extension of time in the very words he himself has used with the king: 'Have patience with me, and I will pay you.' But with an extraordinary lack of compassion, he brutally seizes his debtor 'by the throat'. Even worse, he refuses to allow the unfortunate man any further time but has him flung straightaway into prison.

The king, when he learns of this cruel and merciless incident, summons back the unforgiving servant and angrily revokes the pardon that has been granted. The unforgiving servant will now be tortured until he repays the entire gigantic debt that he has incurred. Remembering the astronomical amount he owes, we may well ask ourselves: No matter how the torture drives him to search out some solution, when will he ever be able to pay back what he owes?

To bring out the wonderfully tender love of God, Jesus tells us the story of the lovingly compassionate father of the prodigal son. But the same Jesus also portrays his and our heavenly Father as a fierce and powerful king who demands that we forgive our brothers and sisters from our heart. It is with utter seriousness that the parable of the unforgiving servant urges us to show mercy to those who sin against us. God sets an astounding standard of mercy and expects us to imitate this example in our own lives.

The unforgiving servant fails to marvel at the extraordinary generosity with which the king treats him. Here this ungrateful person shows himself staggeringly different from a chief tax collector in Luke's Gospel. Zacchaeus behaves in the way the servant should have behaved. Overcome by the generous forgiveness he has received, Zacchaeus tells Jesus: 'Half of my possessions, Lord, I will give to the poor; and if I have defrauded anyone of anything, I will pay back four times as much' (Luke 19:8).

THE PATRIARCH JOSEPH AND MODERN EXAMPLES

In recent years I gave myself a refresher course in the Old Testament by watching a whole series of films on biblical characters produced by a joint American–Italian enterprise. The films took me through the stories of Noah, Abraham and Sarah, Jacob and Rachel, Moses, Samson and Delilah, and right on down to the life of King David. One of the most moving moments in all that viewing came with the climax in the story of the patriarch Joseph. His brothers, who have treated him cruelly and then sold him into slavery, find themselves alone with the powerful prime minister of Egypt, who is none other than Joseph. The camera sweeps from trembling face to trembling face. They cannot bring themselves to believe that, after all they did to him, Joseph has forgiven them and loves them.

Right to the very end of the Book of Genesis, Joseph's brothers are still terrified that he has not truly forgiven them. He may have buried the hatchet for the moment. But he must have carefully marked the spot. Now that their father Jacob is dead and buried, Joseph will dig up the hatchet and finally have his revenge. With tears filling his eyes, Joseph once again assures his brothers that he has truly forgiven them and will always take care of them (Genesis 50:15–21). Both the biblical story of Joseph and, in its own visual way, the American–Italian film highlight the great challenge which forgiveness presents.

In one of his novels, Jean-Paul Sartre caricatures a happy character who could see no difficulty about forgiveness. He believed that the only thing needed to settle all conflicts was a little common sense. If only it were as easy as that!

Our world desperately needs forgiveness between whole nations and large groups who continue to savage and kill each other with irrational ferocity. But we cannot expect forgiveness on a grand scale between peoples and races if we fail to practise it on a small scale in our own lives.

G.K. Chesterton once remarked, 'I find it easy to love Eskimos, because I have never seen an Eskimo. But I find it hard to love my neighbour who plays the piano over my head too late at night.' We all have something to forgive in others, perhaps much to forgive, and it won't be as trifling as someone on the floor above us who plays the piano into the night. It may be our parents who need our forgiveness. It could be someone who has persistently treated us as if we were a thing and not a person. It may be the case of friends and close relatives who have betrayed us. Forgiveness is difficult and costly.

I think here of an Anglican bishop in northern Uganda, whose wife was killed by a landmine in 1997. In his diocese, 78 out of 80 places for worship have been destroyed, damaged or forced to be abandoned by mindless terrorist activity. Far from indulging bitter anger over his tragic losses, the bishop goes on working to bring forgiveness and peace to his tormented country.

Over the last year another African has delivered to me the same message almost day by day. Very often I take breakfast with a tall Tutsi priest, many of whose close relatives and friends were hacked to death in the genocidal massacres of 1994. His gentle, compassionate attitude constantly makes me think: 'How can I ever dare even to think that someone has treated me badly when Theo shows such loving forgiveness?'

Living in Rome through the late 1970s and into the early 1980s made me sadly conscious of the senseless and cruel killings carried out by members of the Red Brigade, the First Line and other terrorist organizations. At the same time, the funeral services of their victims over and over again revealed the power God gave to grief-stricken people to forgive and show mercy.

On 30 May 1980, at the funeral of Walter Tobagi, a young journalist assassinated by the Red Brigade in revenge for what he had written about them, Archbishop (later Cardinal) Carlo Maria Martini of Milan spoke of a 'mystery of meaninglessness and madness'. But then he reminded his congregation of that great certainty Jesus brings: 'What is meaningless can gain a meaning.' The prayers of the faithful which followed the Archbishop's homily showed most movingly how Jesus can help those in terrible sorrow to see meaning in what they experience and to express forgiveness and love. Stella Tobagi, left widowed with her two little children, had written this prayer and sat with her arms around her son and daughter while her sister read it:

Lord, we pray for those who killed Walter, and for all people who wrongly hold that violence is the only way for resolving problems. May the power of your Spirit change the hearts of men, and out of Walter's death may there be born a hope which the force of arms will never be able to defeat.

Stella Tobagi, no less than the Ugandan bishop and the Tutsi priest, showed us a follower of Jesus who forgives from the heart.

GIVING AND FORGIVING

None of these great Christians would pretend that forgiveness is easy. In their own way our languages make this very point. To 'forgive', like the French *pardonner*, the German *vergeben* and the Italian *perdonare*, is a longer and strengthened form of the verb 'give'. It sounds as though forgiving is giving to the power of 'n' – in fact until seventy times seven times, as Jesus himself put it (Matthew 18:21–2). To give to others is not always easy; to forgive them can be much harder, even heroic. Our Lord has sometimes been described as 'the man born to give'. He could be described even better as 'the man born to forgive'. Those who see the high point of his parables, other teaching and whole ministry as loving mercy, forgiveness and reconciliation argue a good case.

Jesus struck his contemporary critics as scandalous in a number of things he said and did. Nowhere did they see him more scandalously generous than in his readiness to forgive. Here they found him dangerously permissive. If there is to be any area where love should make us 'permissive', it is in this matter of forgiving others. Jesus showed himself the utter opposite of the unforgiving debtor. We would be horrified even to imagine him seizing someone by the throat and instantly demanding his rights. He was patient and magnanimous to an extreme. He has left us the challenge of following him in his way of forgiveness.

Matthew's Gospel provides us with the longer, familiar form of the 'Our Father', in which we praise God and then ask for ourselves: 'Forgive us our debts, as we also have forgiven our debtors' (Matthew 6:12). Luke's form of the Lord's Prayer is shorter but does not fail to include forgiveness, that essential point in Jesus' programme for the kingdom: 'Forgive us our sins, for we ourselves forgive everyone indebted to us' (Luke 11:4). Nothing shows more clearly God's merciful love towards us than the divine forgiveness. Nothing shows more clearly our love towards others than our willingness to forgive others from our heart.

This is the one point where Jesus expects us to testify before God what we are doing. The 'Our Father' does not propose that we pray: 'Give us this day our daily bread, as we give their daily bread to others', or 'Lead us not into temptation, just as we refrain from leading others into temptation.' The only point which calls for personal testimony about our own attitudes and performances is forgiveness: 'Forgive us our trespasses as we forgive those who trespass against us.'

The parable of the unforgiving servant puts into relief God's greatness and our littleness. Over against the mind-boggling debt owed to the king, £2,250,000,000, any-thing that might be owed to us is as small as the debt of £6,000. The parable also supplies an alternate prayer for those who wel-come Jesus' message and stake their lives on the coming of God's kingdom. On our knees we could well pray: 'O God, have patience with me, even as I want to always have patience with others.'

A Prayer

Deliver us, O God, from meanness, malice and an
unforgiving spirit.
Give us the grace to pardon all who have offended us,
and to bear with one another,
even as you, Lord, bear with us in your great patience
and loving kindness.

Exercises

1 Why does Jesus insist so strongly on our need to be merci-ful and forgiving?
2 What can make forgiveness very hard?
3 How can we be helped to have a more forgiving spirit?

CHAPTER ELEVEN

THE GOOD SAMARITAN

A lawyer stood up to test Jesus. 'Teacher,' he said, 'what must I do to inherit eternal life?' He said to him, 'What is written in the law? What do you read there?' He answered, 'You shall love the Lord your God with all your heart, and with all your soul, and with all your strength, and with all your mind, and your neighbour as yourself.' And he said to him, 'You have given the right answer; do this, and you will live.'

But wanting to justify himself, the lawyer asked Jesus, 'And who is my neighbour?' Jesus replied, 'A man was going down from Jerusalem to Jericho, and fell into the hands of robbers, who stripped him, beat him, and went away, leaving him half dead. Now by chance a priest was going down that road; and when he saw him, he passed by on the other side. So likewise a levite, when he came to the place and saw him, passed by on the other side. But a Samaritan while travelling came near him, and when he saw him, he was moved to pity. He went to him and bandaged his wounds, having poured oil and wine on them. Then he put him on his own animal, brought him to an inn, and took care of him. The next day he took out two denarii, gave them to the innkeeper, and said, "Take care of him; and when I come back, I will repay you whatever more you spend." Which of these three, do you think, was a neighbour to the man who fell into the hands of the robbers?' He said, 'The one who showed him mercy.' Jesus said to him, 'Go and do likewise.'

(Luke 10:25–37)

The parable of the unforgiving servant bears down on something that can be a challenge day by day: Jesus' call to show at home, at our workplace, in our church and everywhere a patient, merciful spirit. The story we look at in this chapter proposes an emergency situation. In most countries it is not a daily occurrence to come across a naked man who has been robbed and left wounded on the side of the road. It does happen, but fortunately is not a frequent event

AN UNUSUAL STORY

The naming of this parable is also unusual. After all, the lawyer whose question prompts Jesus into telling the story asks about the object of his and our loving concern: 'Who is my neighbour?' Instead of being called 'The Parable of the Wounded Traveller' after someone who is obviously a striking case of a neighbour desperately needing help, the story has become known in terms of the Samaritan, the outsider whose generous concern turns him into the central character.

This somewhat unexpected naming of the parable corresponds, of course, to the unexpected way in which Jesus develops the story. Instead of concentrating on the example of someone who cries out for our help, in a surprising way Jesus speaks about the agent of neighbourly love for those in critical situations, who need our intensive care. He not only switches from the object to the agent of love, but he also gets in a strong plug against religious and racial discrimination.

Like so many of Jesus' parables, this story does not explicitly introduce God. It looks thoroughly secular and this-worldly. At most, the mention of a priest and a levite, both connected with the divine service in the Jerusalem temple, hints at God and the other world. But, unlike what he does in all the parables we have so far looked at, Jesus does not talk vaguely of a 'distant country', a vineyard located somewhere or other, and a treasure that turns up in some field. In this case Jesus locates his story very precisely: on the road from Jerusalem to Jericho. Its exact geography delighted me on my first visit to Israel. Let me explain.

As an Australian I was happy to notice a special little link with my own country that came from the location Jesus gave his story. All over the Holy Land, Australian gum-trees offer shade and sweeten the air. They flank the road that leads across the Plain of Esdraclon towards Nazareth. They give shelter on the Mount of the Beatitudes, and fill the ground between the ruins of Capernaum and the Sea of Galilee. At the bend in the Jordan where many pilgrims enter the water to renew their baptismal vows, gum-trees tower over the river and fill the air with the scent of eucalyptus. When you take the road going down from Jerusalem to Jericho, you run across an ancient stone enclosure, called the Good Samaritan Inn. It tops a rise and looks across folding valleys, where over the centuries bandits often concealed themselves and lay in wait for victims to rob. On my visit there I saw, right outside the inn, a chunky gumtree which offers the traveller a little relief from the heat and the flies. I was encouraged to find an Australian tree making its mark alongside a road mentioned by Jesus in one of his most memorable parables.

JOKES AND STORIES

Many people have jokes and stories to tell when you mention the parable of the good Samaritan. From years ago I recall the crowds who attended a particular parish church on Good Samaritan Sunday, a day in the year when this story provided the reading at the Gospel. The particular attraction came from the combative parish priest, who insisted on identifying the priest, the levite and the good Samaritan with people living at the time in Sydney. 'Despite those who reported me to the cathedral authorities last year,' he would announce, 'I still identify the priest with our archbishop.'

Around that same time I remember one evening in Sydney walking down a suburban street with one of my sisters and a female cousin of ours. A man was sitting on the footpath, his feet dangling into the gutter and his body gently swaying backwards and forwards. The smell of spirits caught us as we walked by. Half an hour later the three of us came back along the same street. An ambulance crew was loading the man on board. He was drunk all right. But he had been sitting down because a car had hit him, breaking his leg, and had failed to stop.

'It's the good Samaritan story,' my sister commented. 'Only this time, instead of a priest and a levite passing by on the other side, it's been us three: a priest, a social worker and a nurse passing by on the same side.' At least she wasn't as hard on my profession as the man who once said to me: 'You know why the priest didn't cross the road to the wounded traveller? He could see that he had already been robbed.'

BACK TO JESUS

Jesus draws his story right out of Palestinian Jewish society. Presumably the unfortunate traveller who is leaving the heights of Jerusalem for the plains of Jericho and on the way runs into a bunch of bandits is a Jew. One may also presume that the priest has been serving in the temple and is returning to his wife and family. The levite is likewise hurrying home, after assisting priests at worship and attending to other services in the temple. Yet the story catches us and – we can imagine – Jesus' original audience off guard.

Obviously there is nothing surprising about adopting the traditional scheme of three characters. Yet one might expect Jesus to name as neighbours three people who live near by: say, a person right next door, someone who lives down the street, and then some chap I work with. He could have said: 'You must show love to the woman in the next house who shouts at her children, to the wretched tax collector who works for Herod

Antipas and the Roman authorities, and to the lazy chap who works in the same vineyard as you do.' Instead Jesus takes us right out of our town or village, and wants us to think of people travelling along a dangerous country road. He jolts his audience further, as we observed above, by introducing not three objects of our neighbourly love but three people who are abruptly faced with a situation in which they might exercise such love.

Jesus, without any doubt, must have taken aback his first audience (and not just the lawyer who was speaking with him) even more by introducing a priest, a levite *and a Samaritan*. Jesus was a layman, known to be somewhat anticlerical. Despite their privileged and respected status, he had so far never given anyone from the religious establishment a role in any of his extraordinary stories. He preferred to talk about farmers and their sons, agricultural labourers, housewives, shepherds, rulers, servants working for wealthy folk, merchants on journeys, widows and judges. So Jesus' audience may not have been flabbergasted to find that, when he did something exceptional and gave a 'walk-on' role to two men from the religious establishment, he put them in a bad light. But those in that audience must have expected that a kind Jewish layman would be the third to come down the road and then take care of the wounded man. 'We knew he was going to say that,' they would then have told themselves. Instead they were dumbfounded to hear Jesus send a Samaritan down the road.

It's all so improbable. What's a hated Samaritan doing travelling (also apparently alone) in Judea? In today's terms, it sounds like a member of the Serbian police force driving along a country road near Zagreb and stopping to take loving care of an injured Croat. But, to everyone's astonishment, Jesus names a Samaritan as the person who 'came near' to the wounded man and 'was moved to pity'.

Far from even coming near, not to speak of being moved to pity, both the priest and the levite pass by quickly 'on the other side'. Jesus probably doesn't need to explain the motivation behind the failure in neighbourly love on the part of those two. The robbers have left the wounded man naked, unconscious or only semi-conscious. He cannot even cry out for help; for anyone who is going by hurriedly, he looks like a corpse. Contact with a dead body will defile the priest and levite; they cannot afford to let themselves become unclean and so unfit for God's holy service. They feel themselves obliged to head on as fast as possible.

It's left to the Samaritan outsider, whom no one expected to stop for a wounded Jew, to give the intensive care desperately needed by someone who would otherwise die. He is 'moved to pity', just like Jesus when he sees a leper (Mark 1:41) and a great crowd who seem to be 'sheep without a shepherd' (Mark 6:34). The Samaritan gives himself to the wounded traveller. Conceivably he might have pressed on down the hill to the inn and told the innkeeper: 'Look, there's a chap lying by the roadside back there. Here's some money to get him picked up and cared for.' Instead the Samaritan himself provides the 'ambulance service'.

He is carrying some oil and wine – one presumes as provisions for snacks along the way. But now they serve to clean and soothe the wounds of the one victimized by the robbers. The Samaritan uses some cloth to make bandages. Does he tear up a change of clothing he is carrying in his baggage? Having done the best he can at the side of the road, he heaves the wounded man on to the animal he was riding and walks along with him to the next inn. He has brought the wounded man to a secure place. In the story, the inn naturally stands for safety, shelter and further care.

What some readers of the parable consider surprising is the way the Samaritan is trusted. He spends the night with the wounded man; before leaving on the following morning, he tells the Judean innkeeper: 'Take care of him; and when I come back, I will repay you whatever more you spend.' The innkeeper finds himself dealing with a despised or even hated outsider, a Samaritan. But he behaves with the hospitality and openness characteristic of good innkeepers everywhere and at all times. On the scale of human kindness towards those in great distress, the innkeeper belongs at one end, not far behind the Good Samaritan himself. Even if one cannot say that he displays the extraordinary generosity of the Samaritan, the innkeeper does well in welcoming the wounded man and trusting the Samaritan to return and pay for any further expenses.

Jesus ends the parable by putting a question to the man whose question has occasioned the telling of the story: 'Who was a neighbour to the man who fell into the hands of the robbers?' It is a vivid and plausible touch when the Jewish lawyer studiously avoids saying 'the Samaritan'. He cannot bring himself to name one of those 'horrible' religious schismatics and social outcasts, but simply answers: 'The one who showed him mercy'. Delicious irony peeps through. On the one hand, a precise expression, 'the good Samaritan', here enters as such into world history and numerous languages to describe for all time anyone who shows remarkable benevolence to those in terrible trouble. The 'good Samaritan' creates the role and becomes a household word. On the other hand, the Jewish lawyer himself begins the very process of generalizing the point of the parable. Whether they are Samaritans, Jews, Koreans, Scots, Croats, Spaniards, Italians, or any other nationality, neighbours are all those who 'show mercy' towards people in terrible trouble. Neighbours are those who go beyond the boundaries of their ethnic or religious groups to care for the suffering whom they meet on their way through life.

A DOUBLE MESSAGE

The very last words of the whole passage, 'Go and do likewise', take us beyond any original setting for the parable to a feature of St Luke's writing. This evangelist has the habit of introducing doublets, two passages that match each other and clarify each other. Over and over again in Luke's Gospel and his Book of Acts we come across such doublets: section A which says something important to us, and then section B which adds something equally important to fill out what we have already read in section A.

Luke alerts us to an example of such doublets when he introduces two distinct stories with the very same question, 'what must I do to inherit eternal life?' (Luke 10:25; 18:18). The first story is the one concerned with the Jewish lawyer, who prompts Jesus into telling the parable of the Good Samaritan. At the end the lawyer is told, '*Go* and do likewise.'[1] In the second story Jesus invites a ruler to give up all he has to the poor and then '*Come*, follow me.' The identical question produces two seemingly different answers. The first man is sent away to care for wounded travellers and any other human beings in distress. The second is called to get rid of his possessions and spend his time, even his life, in the company of Jesus. But on closer scrutiny the two invitations can be seen to complement and support each other rather than proving to be mutually exclusive. Those who live in loving and prayerful familiarity with Jesus will have the strength to go and imitate the selfless compassion of the good Samaritan. Those who generously serve their neighbours will do so because prayer has shown them the face of Jesus himself in the sick, prisoners, refugees, the old and the dying. They can *do* 'something beautiful' for Jesus, because they have looked on his face in prayer.

In sharing with us this double message, Luke relates to Jesus what has emerged in the exchange with the Jewish lawyer that introduces the good Samaritan story: 'You shall love the Lord your God with all your heart, and with all your soul, and with all your strength, and with all your mind; and your neighbour as yourself' (Luke 10:27). Jesus gives his approval to this linking of the two commands of love towards God and towards one's neighbour. On the one hand, loving God with all our heart will fuel practical kindness towards our brothers and sisters. On the other hand, such kindness will prove itself through enduring practice because it springs from a prayerful love for the Lord our God. Even though, as we have seen, the parable of the good Samaritan itself does not explicitly mention God, its setting in Luke's Gospel encourages us to read it as part of a double message – of love towards God and towards one's neighbour.

GOOD SAMARITANS AND INNKEEPERS

Personal cost and personal risk belong right in the story Jesus told. The good Samaritan's kindness cost him some oil, wine, clothing and money – as well as the loss of time caused by the unforeseen break in his journey. We shouldn't miss also the slight whiff of danger: if one traveller had been robbed, bandits could still have been prowling around to attack and rob others. It was dangerous to stop at the side of the road and then move slowly ahead keeping the wounded man from falling off his seat on the animal.

Recently I was told of an Anglican missionary who was asked not just to visit but also to lay his hands on and anoint a man suffering from advanced leprosy. Before going to do so, he asked a doctor about the chances of infection. 'I am talking to you as a Christian,' the doctor replied. 'Please go and do it.' The story evoked for me the memory of a nineteenth-century Belgian missionary who worked in the islands of Hawaii and was so vigorously defended by Robert Louis Stevenson. Father Damien volunteered to serve lepers on the island of Molokai. He worked there for sixteen years as pastor, doctor, sheriff and undertaker. Eventually he contracted leprosy himself but continued working until a month before his death in 1889. As I write this chapter (in January 1999) I have just read a report of a missionary burned to death with his two small sons. For over thirty years he had lived away from his home country and taken care of lepers in his land of adoption.

When I went to high school, one of my companions had already lost his father, a doctor who during the war had remained behind on an island to care for the sick in the hospital, although he could have been evacuated with the other civilians. When an invading force arrived, they executed him. Many of us will have stories like that to tell: of pastors refusing to abandon high-crime areas and eventually paying for their devotion with their lives; of nurses stopping to care for a wounded person shot by some berserk young man and then being gunned down themselves; of aid workers coming home in a coffin.

At the Gregorian University in Rome I live and teach at a great crossroads of the world. Over and over again I am amazed and encouraged by the heroic generosity of students who finish their studies with us and leave for posts that put them constantly in danger. They spend their whole lives out there on a kind of Jerusalem to Jericho road, and do not merely travel such a dangerous road occasionally. Recently a woman student returned on holiday; her work on the Amazon has left her cheerfully alive but weakened by hepatitis.

In the mid-1980s Sister Luz Marina Valencia Treviño, a nun from Columbia, attended the Gregorian University for three years and gained her 'licence' or advanced master's degree in missionary theology. Before coming to Rome, she had already been working for very poor people in Venezuela. After receiving her degree in mid-1986, she left for Acapulco and joined a pastoral team in an utterly destitute parish of that Mexican archdiocese. A powerful family owned the land, exploited the farm workers, and paid their *peons* a dreadful pittance. On the night of 20 March 1987, four men armed with revolvers broke into the cottage where Luz Marina lived. After beating and raping her, they shot her in the stomach and left her in agony. She died after suffering for seven hours and forgiving her murderers. In his tribute to Luz Marina, the Archbishop first stressed her day by day fidelity to God's grace before he named her 'the first martyr of Acapulco'. The pastoral team with which she had worked declared: 'In her life and death she witnessed to the gospel values and the dignity of women.' She was only thirty-four when she died, a modern good Samaritan who stopped to help wounded people and paid the ultimate price for her neighbourly love.

Before we end this chapter, we would do well to think of the life of Jesus himself and do so in two ways. First of all, some things link him to the silent innkeeper. Let me explain. Luke's Gospel begins with the conception and birth of Jesus: when he is born, Mary could find no room 'in the inn (*kataluma*)' (Luke 2:7). Then during his ministry Jesus told one of his most memorable parables which featured a thoroughly hospitable innkeeper. At the end, in Luke's Gospel Jesus celebrated the passover with his core group of disciples in a *kataluma*, or inn (Luke 22:11). After not enjoying at his birth the normal welcome, Jesus not only put a friendly innkeeper into one of his most remarkable stories but also at the end offered his friends unique hospitality in a Jerusalem 'inn'. Naturally, in Luke 22 our attention focuses on the institution of the Lord's Supper and our enduring experience of Jesus in the Eucharist. But we can and should *also* interpret the command 'do this in remembrance of me' in terms of welcoming hospitality. At the Last Supper, Jesus also plays an exquisite role as 'the' Innkeeper, and invites us to remember and follow him in that role.

Jesus the Innkeeper does not crowd out his role as Jesus the Good Samaritan. Once again one of his parables turns out to be vividly autobiographical. His life dramatizes his story. At his own personal cost and risk, he stops to save wounded beings who have been robbed and stripped. In this case, however, love for his neighbours costs much more than possessions, money and time. Jesus as the good Samaritan will himself be stripped and wounded. He will turn into Jesus the Victimized Traveller, not rescued but left to die on the cross.

A PRAYER

O God, to love you is our destiny and life itself.
Open our hearts to all who need our concern and help.
Help us to minister to those who do not belong to 'our'
    group,
and make us always compassionate to the wounded and
    suffering.

EXERCISES

1 Please share with others your stories about good Samaritans whose love for those in distress cost them much.
2 Do cheerful and welcoming pub-owners remind you of Jesus?
3 Does the story we read in Matthew 25:31–46 allow Jesus to challenge us: 'I was wounded and bleeding on the side of the road. Did you stop for me?'

1 The lawyer, we read, wants to 'justify himself'. Presumably we are meant to understand that he is anxious to establish his right to eternal life by specifying exactly the nature of his duty towards his neighbours and then by proving that he has carried it out. In that case he would be shown to be 'righteous' or acceptable to God.

CHAPTER TWELVE

THE RICH MAN AND LAZARUS

There was a rich man who was dressed in purple and fine linen and who feasted sumptuously every day. And at his gate lay a poor man named Lazarus, covered with sores, who longed to satisfy his hunger with what fell from the rich man's table; even the dogs would come and lick his sores. The poor man died and was carried away by the angels to be with Abraham. The rich man also died and was buried. In Hades, where he was being tormented, he looked up and saw Abraham far away with Lazarus by his side. He called out, 'Father Abraham, have mercy on me, and send Lazarus to dip the tip of his finger in water and cool my tongue; for I am in agony in these flames.' But Abraham said, 'Child, remember that during your lifetime you received your good things, and Lazarus in like manner evil things; but now he is comforted here, and you are in agony. Besides all this, between you and us a great chasm has been fixed, so that those who might want to pass from here to you cannot do so, and no one can cross from there to us.' He said, 'Then, father, I beg you to send him to my father's house – for I have five brothers – that he may warn them, so that they will not also come into this place of torment.' Abraham replied, 'They have Moses and the prophets; they should listen to them.' He said, 'No, Father Abraham; but if someone goes to them from the dead, they will repent.' He said to him, 'If they do not listen to Moses and the prophets, neither will they be convinced even if someone rises from the dead.'

(Luke 16:19–31)

The case of the good Samaritan confronts us with an emergency situation; it is not every day that we run into a desperately wounded person whose life depends on our compassionate concern. The story of the rich man and Lazarus opens, however, with a scene repeated day by day in many cities of our world: wealthy, well-dressed people dining lavishly in their grand homes and apartments, while beggars lie outside in the streets with rags covering their ulcerated bodies.[1] In his words about the rich man and Lazarus, Jesus brought up a challenge that recurs constantly. As Jesus said in another context: 'You always have the poor with you, and you can show kindness to them whenever you wish' (Mark 14:7). The words sting our consciences: How often do we show them kindness? What stops us from wishing to do that and then going into action?

The parables of the good Samaritan and the rich man and Lazarus envisage different situations but converge in driving home the same basic programme of behaviour. Those who accept Jesus' message of the kingdom must actively reach out to their brothers and sisters in need. The two stories join in providing terrifying insight into our deep tendency to indulge and even justify selfish unconcern.

The two stories move apart, however, through their geography and their protagonists. The good Samaritan story takes place very much in this world – in fact, along a road used by thousands of people right down to the present day. The story of the rich man and Lazarus begins in some unnamed town and then moves off into the other world, with Lazarus being 'carried away by the angels' and 'receiving good things' at the side of Abraham, and the rich man 'being tormented' in Hades. We shift from a street on this earth to the world of the angels and Abraham, a world that looks across 'a great chasm' to the 'place of torment'.

The characters Jesus puts into the good Samaritan story belong very much to the world of daily experience: an unfortunate traveller, some robbers, a priest, a minor cleric, another traveller and an innkeeper. The story of the rich man and Lazarus brings in angels and, above all, Abraham as protagonists. The angels may have, so to speak, only 'fly-on' parts, but Abraham has a notable speaking role in the dialogue that makes up more than half the story. In fact, this is the longest dialogue in any of Jesus' parables. In other stories such as those of the prodigal son and the labourers in the vineyard, Jesus injects some striking dialogue. But nowhere else does such dialogue include any otherworldly figures, let alone the patriarch Abraham who was called with his wife Sarah to initiate the story of the people of God.

Abraham enters the story by name, and so too does the poor man. In the parable of the good Samaritan and all the stories that Jesus left us, the only earthly figure who has a name is Lazarus. Elsewhere Jesus simply speaks of 'robbers', 'a priest', 'a judge', 'a widow', or merely of 'a man' or 'a woman'. Why does he give the poor man a name? Some scholars have seen in this story a discreet hint of the raising from the dead of Jesus' friend from Bethany, Lazarus (John 11:1–44). He is brought back to life but, far from convincing the powerful enemies of Jesus, the episode prompts their decision to do away with Jesus (John 11:46–53) and even to kill Lazarus (John 12:10). What John's Gospel relates goes beyond the story from Luke 16, which faces the issue of convincing or not convincing the rich man's five brothers to change their way of life and so avoid finishing up in Hades. Jesus' story as reported by Luke in no way even insinuates that someone's return from the dead would trigger off a double killing. Such a sign, as Abraham warns, won't have any effect at all. The rich man's five brothers will not be brought to repentance by someone coming to them from the dead. Whether or not Luke's Lazarus story should be linked with the Lazarus of John 11, the common name invites us to compare and contrast the two texts – both of them very dramatic in their own different ways.

JESUS' STORY

Having 'placed' the account of the rich man and Lazarus in relation to other stories from Jesus, let us look at some of its details. The story makes not the slightest suggestion that the rich man has gained his wealth by immoral or even criminal practices. He is not pictured as engaging in shady deals like the dishonest manager (see Chapter 7 above). The rich man's sin is one of omission: although he has the money to be elegantly dressed and extremely well fed every day, he ignores a destitute person who would have been satisfied to eat the leftovers from the lavish feasts. He fails by the standards Jesus spells out: 'I was hungry and you gave me food; I was naked and you gave me clothing' (Matthew 25:35–6).

Jesus portrays a painful contrast. The rich man dresses in the most expensive clothing and presumably has many friends, as well as his five brothers and other relatives, to gorge themselves at his table. Lazarus is 'dressed' in his sores. No one comes to do anything for him except some dogs. Where human beings fail in their duty of loving concern, the animals at least do what they can; by licking the sores of Lazarus, they give him some relief. The rich man enjoys nothing but 'good things', whereas Lazarus has almost nothing but 'evil things'.

The dreadful contrast continues after death, but now in a strikingly reversed shape. The story dramatically expresses what we have read earlier in the same Gospel of Luke:

Blessed are you who are poor, for yours is the kingdom of God. Blessed are you who are hungry now, for you will be filled. Blessed are you who weep now, for you will laugh ... But woe to you who are rich, for you have received your consolation. Woe to you who are full now, for you will be hungry. Woe to you who are laughing now, for you will mourn and weep.

(Luke 6:20–1, 24–5)

Right at the start of Luke's Gospel, the Magnificat praises God who 'has filled the hungry with good things and sent the rich away empty' (Luke 1:53).

The poor, hungry Lazarus is carried away by angels to be 'comforted' in Abraham's bosom: that is to say, in the life to come he enjoys a choice position at the heavenly, messianic banquet. The rich, well-fed man dies and is 'buried', an ominous word that receives immediate clarification: he has gone down to be tormented in the underworld. When he looks up, he sees, far above him, Lazarus at the side of Abraham. In his tragic situation the rich man now needs a little help from Lazarus, the very person he has cruelly neglected during life on earth. He pleads piteously with Abraham: 'Send Lazarus to dip the tip of his finger in water and cool my tongue; for I am in agony in these flames.'

But, as Abraham stresses, Lazarus and the rich man are now separated. During their earthly existence they lived a very short distance from each other. The rich man could very easily and quickly have brought or sent some food, clothing and medicine to Lazarus. Now, however, 'a great chasm' keeps the two men apart. It is impossible for them to meet. Even if Lazarus wants to perform some tiny act of kindness for the tormented rich man, a great chasm is now in place and separates them. It is impossible to cross from one side to the other.

In his dreadful misery, the rich man asks Abraham to send Lazarus back to his house and family. The rich man's five brothers will surely listen to someone risen from the dead, repent of their selfish life and, presumably, begin to use their wealth to help the utterly destitute. They will stop living in a callous, self-centred way and think of others who desperately need their help.

But Abraham sweeps aside the idea. The five brothers have the guidance and motivation provided by their religion; in particular, their scriptures offer a strong message from Moses and the prophets about our duty towards those in terrible want. If they fail to hear that message, they will not pay attention to someone who comes to them from beyond the grave. To say the least, the five brothers do not lack abundant spiritual directives and help. Will even the striking sign of a resurrection from the dead shake them out of their decadent and self-absorbed style of living?

A FINAL CONTRAST

Active, loving concern towards the impoverished and afflicted belongs up front in Jesus' programme for those who accept his message of the divine kingdom. He depicts two men faced with persons in terrible distress. The good Samaritan seems moderately well off. He may be travelling alone and without any servants, but he is riding on an animal, perhaps only a donkey rather than a hefty mule or horse. He carries some provisions and has at least a little spare cash. He does everything he can for the wounded victim of robbers. The wealthy man seems very affluent, but he does nothing for the starving Lazarus, who is lying not some distance off down the road but right there at the entrance to the rich house.

Why does the good Samaritan act and the rich man remain coolly indifferent? Perhaps the latter's extraordinary opulence has corrupted him. Or is the rich man a professionally religious person who uses the 'right' words but fails to live out his faith? Three times he uses such 'right' words in his dialogue with Abraham, calling him 'Father Abraham', 'father', and 'Father Abraham'. What we read here may well remind us of John the Baptist's stinging rebuke to those who boasted of having Abraham as their father: 'Bear fruits worthy of repentance' (Luke 3:8). This language also challenges me as a Roman Catholic; in our First Eucharistic Prayer, the old Roman Canon, the priest recalls Abraham as 'our father in faith'. The story of the rich man and Lazarus highlights the fact that mere religious words about Abraham and faith will not be enough. We will be 'known by our fruits' (Matthew 7:20).

The rich man knows his religion, from Abraham and Moses on to all the classical prophets. He enjoys extensive financial resources. He has so much, yet does nothing. In his own way this rich man comments on the servant who receives five talents from his employer. Despite that 'successful' figure being praised highly in the parable of the talents, those who receive much may not necessarily do anything significant with what they receive. After all, in the good Samaritan story the priest and the levite, for all the advantages of their religious profession, don't lift a finger to help the wounded traveller. They 'see' the victim, but not in the sense of truly seeing him in his need and feeling effective compassion for him (Luke 10:32–3).

The good Samaritan story says nothing about the religious profession and practice of the central protagonist. His only words concern arrangements with the innkeeper about help for the wounded person: 'Take care of him; and when I come back, I will repay you whatever more you spend.' To be sure, the story does not deny the good Samaritan's faith in God, let alone represent him as being a first-century atheist or agnostic. A loving relationship with God should obviously be presumed by the opening exchange between Jesus and the lawyer – an exchange which puts right up front loving God with all our heart. But in the parable itself the good Samaritan acts instantly with spectacular generosity when he finds himself suddenly faced with a near-tragic emergency. He acts rather than indulging some empty professions of faith.

A Prayer

> O God our merciful Father, you look with special love on the destitute and homeless.
> Open our hearts to care constantly for distressed and suffering people.
> Turn us all into good Samaritans as we make our way along the road to your heavenly kingdom.

EXERCISES

1 What would *you* include in a full comparison and contrast
   between the good Samaritan and the rich man?
2 The rich man's five brothers should listen to Moses and the
   prophets. What else should *we* be listening to when we seek
   to live lives worthy of Jesus' call to the kingdom?

1 Recently an old friend told me of a large capital city which has an
   impressive hospital for animals. Outside the building hungry and dying
   beggars lie in the streets.

CHAPTER THIRTEEN

THE WIDOW AND THE UNJUST JUDGE

Then Jesus told them a parable about their need to pray always and not to lose heart. He said, 'In a certain city there was a judge who neither feared God nor had respect for people. In that city there was a widow who kept coming to him and saying, "Grant me justice against my opponent." For a while he refused, but later he said to himself, "Though I have no fear of God and no respect for anyone, yet because this widow keeps bothering me, I will grant her justice, so that she may not wear me out by continually coming." ' And the Lord said, 'Listen to what the unjust judge says. And will not God grant justice to his chosen ones who cry to him day and night? Will he delay long in helping them? I tell you, he will quickly grant justice to them. And yet when the Son of Man comes, will he find faith on earth?'

(Luke 18:2–8)

The last two chapters have dealt with horizontal duties for those who follow Jesus. His parables of the good Samaritan and the rich man and Lazarus share with us how he feels about our conduct towards our brothers and sisters in distress. The next two stories take us into Jesus' mind and heart about our behaviour 'vertically', towards our God.

Did Jesus fashion for himself the whole story of the widow and the unjust judge? Did it arise out of his own prayer and imagination? Or had he known cases of widows who suffered hardship at the hands of unjust judges? One ingredient for the creative imagination of Jesus came from his inherited scriptures. The psalmist knows how widows and orphans have no one to defend them; they can all too easily be victimized (Psalm 68:5). In the Book of Ruth we read of Naomi, who loses her husband and two sons to death; as a widow she finds herself in a desperately vulnerable situation (Ruth 1:20–1). Jesus' widow fitted a recurrent Old Testament picture of helpless widows to whom justice is often denied.

Whatever the precise balance in his sources, Jesus has shaped the story of a woman whom an anonymous person has treated badly over some issue, also left unspecified. She is not getting her rights. She may be defenceless and lacking the support of a husband and family, but she never quits appealing for justice, and her persistence wins out in the end. This courageous figure invites our admiration, not our surprise. It is Jesus' use of the other figure in the parable which should astonish us. It is 'bad enough' to find Jesus using a dishonest manager to depict our appropriate response when receiving the call of the kingdom. Here, however, Jesus goes much further and has recourse to an unjust judge to depict God. Or at least Jesus compares God to such a figure. The Old Testament parades before us many judges, both men and women (see Judges 4:1–5:31). The biblical role of judges is that of adjudicating disputes between people, rescuing the innocent and injured parties, and punishing the wicked (Exodus 18:13–26). The Book of Deuteronomy vigorously insists on the proper administration of justice: 'Justice, and only justice, you shall pursue' (16:20). The Jewish scriptures have much to say about good and bad judges, but never even approach the boldness of Jesus in associating God with an unjust judge. This key aspect of the parable comes through clearly as Jesus' own contribution.

PERSISTENCE WINS

After the headlines, let us now look at the small print. The theme of 'justice' runs through the story. First, the widow wants justice against her opponent; then the judge eventually decides to grant her justice. Finally, 'the Lord' asks the rhetorical question: 'Will not God grant justice to his chosen ones?', and answers it at once: 'He will grant justice to them.' The widow, the judge and 'the Lord' all speak of 'justice'. Clearly we begin with social justice, in the sense of the widow's public rights being upheld. But when it turns up twice in the mouth of 'the Lord', the term more than hints at the loving fidelity of the just God towards those who turn to him in their needs and sufferings, whatever they are.

The immorality of the judge also forms another thread in the story. First, we are told that he 'feared neither God nor had respect for people'. Then we overhear a soliloquy in which the very words of this pen-portrait become his own brazen self-description: 'I have no fear of God and no respect for anyone.' Finally, to make sure that we know the kind of person the widow has to deal with, 'the Lord' sums him up as a rascal: 'the unjust judge'. Why is the judge, to begin with, unwilling to secure the widow's rights and pronounce against her opponent? In this particular case at least, no corruption seems to be involved; the story does not even hint at any collusion between the judge and her opponent. It appears that the judge couldn't care less about the rights and wrongs of the widow's complaint; he is simply too lazy and dilatory to do anything.

The widow cannot exert any family or group influence on those in power. Persistence is her only weapon. For an indefinite time she keeps coming back to demand her rights, and finally succeeds in undermining the judge's lack of concern for human beings suffering injustice. He wants to be relieved of the burden of her constant complaints. To have peace, he relents, yields to her nagging, hears her case, and grants her justice.

Along with the widow and the judge, Jesus himself speaks within his own story. Luke probably changes the original report he received, 'and Jesus said', to 'the Lord said'. This kind of change has already set in, back at Luke 7:13, in the context of another, different, story about a widow. There, when reporting how Jesus brings back to life the dead son of a widow of Nain, Luke begins to call Jesus 'the Lord'. The Gospel writer maintains faithfully what his sources provide: the people react to the resurrection of the young man by declaring, 'a great prophet has risen among us' (Luke 7:16). But Luke feels that this title is not enough to describe who Jesus is, and starts to give him the name used of God thousands of times in the Jewish scriptures: 'the Lord'. Hence in the parable of the widow and the unjust judge it is 'the Lord' who says, 'Listen to what the unjust judge says. And will not God grant justice to his chosen ones?'

Thus we hear three voices in this parable: those of the widow, the judge and Jesus himself. They each have their say, the judge having more to say than the widow, and Jesus more than the other two combined. As with other such parables, like those of the sower, the talents, and the good Samaritan, a triple scheme organizes the story tightly. The first two voices are those of two antagonists, and the third is that of the commentator who stands outside the action. The commentary sets this story apart from many others that Jesus tells. Normally, as in the story of the prodigal son, he lets the parable speak for itself and does not enter, so to speak, with his own commentary.

Luke's introduction catches well the point of this parable: 'Jesus told them a parable about their need to pray always and not to lose heart.' Persevering prayer should be the mode of life for those who have accepted Jesus' message and as 'chosen ones' entered God's kingdom. The parable builds itself on an 'ever so much more' argument. If the persistent prayer of a weak widow prevails over the laziness of a dishonest judge, how much more ready will the faithful and upright God be to hear the prayers of his people and grant them lasting justice! God will not dilly dally, but will quickly help those in need who cry out to him. Where the judge delays matters for a long time, divine aid will be speedily granted. So far from being like a lazy public official, God is the best of faithful friends and has abundant resources and to spare.

Earlier in Luke's Gospel Jesus has insisted on the need of persistent prayer:

> I say to you, Ask, and it will be given you; search; and you will find; knock, and the door will be opened for you. For everyone who asks receives, and everyone who searches finds; and for everyone who knocks, the door will be opened.
>
> **(Luke 11:9–10)**

This teaching on prayer finds its exemplification in the widow, who never stops asking, searching and knocking, until her suit is heard and her plea upheld.

FAITH ON EARTH

After the parable ends, a question is thrown at us: 'When the Son of Man comes, will he find faith on earth?' Here Jesus, who has just been called 'the Lord', receives another title, 'Son of Man'. When telling the story of the widow and the unjust judge, Jesus may have finished with this question. Or perhaps the Gospel writer has taken this question from somewhere else and added it here. In any case, the question rounds the story off effectively.

The question obviously links prayer and faith. Crying out day and night in prayer comes from faith and will not prove possible without faith. Only those who believe will show staying power in prayer. At the same time, a two-way street operates here. Faith inspires dogged prayer, while persistent praying lets faith grow.

Some scholars rightly connect Jesus' own prayer-life with his personal faith. The Gospels of Matthew, Mark and Luke report that he constantly prayed, even at times spending nights alone in prayer. Very occasionally they take us inside his prayer: for instance, when they all describe his agonized prayer in the garden on the night before he died. What none of them do is to come right out into the open and write of Jesus' own faith. Nevertheless, they make repeated allusions to his life of faith. When Jesus says to the father of the epileptic boy, 'all things are possible for the one who believes' (Mark 9:23), Jesus offers an invitation to share his own faith. Jesus speaks about faith as an insider; he knows through his own experience the power of faith which expresses itself in prayer.

Jesus knows by experience that through people whose faith puts them totally at God's disposition extraordinary results will come. When his disciples ask, 'increase our faith,' he replies: 'If you had faith the size of a mustard seed, you could say to this mulberry tree, "Be uprooted and planted in the sea," and it would obey you' (Luke 17:6). Out of his own faith-life, he knows that even a tiny 'amount' of faith can have astonishing effects. In his encounter with the father of an epileptic boy, Jesus complains about 'this faithless generation' (Mark 9:19). At times he reproaches his disciples as a group and Peter in particular for having 'little faith'. Even when reproving others, Jesus shows how he wants to share with them his faith in their loving God, the Father of boundless mercy and infinite power.

As we saw above, the widow in her dealings with the unjust judge exemplifies wonderfully well Jesus' teaching on prayer. But he himself is surely the paradigm example, the Prayer *par excellence* in the Gospels. He constantly asks, searches and knocks. In faithful prayer he cries out to his God 'day and night', and does so in a most dramatic fashion during the agony in the garden. As we know, through vindicating him in the res-urrection, God did not 'delay long' but 'quickly granted jus-tice' to Jesus, the Chosen One of all chosen ones. Once again, we may read one of the parables in an autobiographical key.

The story of the widow and the unjust judge lets us glimpse something of Jesus' own life and destiny.

The final verse of the story reveals a certain irony that the evangelist Luke has grasped and wants to communicate to his readers. In the previous chapter Jesus declares to those who are waiting for the coming of the divine kingdom: 'the kingdom of God is among you' (Luke 17:21). In and through the person of Jesus himself the reality of the kingdom is already present and available. When we recall how Jesus presents himself constantly, if indirectly, as the Son of Man, we catch the sharp bite in the question: 'When the Son of Man comes, will he find faith on earth?' The Son of Man has come and is there, right in front of his audience. What does he find on earth – faith or a terrible lack of faith? We don't have to wait for his final coming to put the question, but must ask now: What does Jesus find on earth today?

A PRAYER

> With your disciples, Jesus, we pray: 'Increase our faith.'
> Let our faith inspire us to go on searching and knocking
>   in prayer,
> and may this prayer be fruitful in our lives of faith.

EXERCISES

1 Have you ever prayed persistently for someone or something and found your prayer answered?
2 How would you describe the link between faith and prayer?
3 What do you make of giving Jesus two new titles: Jesus the Prayer and Jesus the Believer?

CHAPTER FOURTEEN

THE PHARISEE AND THE TAX COLLECTOR

Two men went up to the temple to pray, one a Pharisee and the other a tax collector. The Pharisee, standing by himself, was praying thus, 'God, I thank you that I am not like other people: thieves, rogues, adulterers, or even like this tax collector. I fast twice a week; I give a tenth of all my income.' But the tax collector, standing far off, would not even look up to heaven, but was beating his breast and saying, 'God, be merciful to me, a sinner!' But I tell you, this man went down to his home justified rather than the other; for all who exalt themselves will be humbled, but all who humble themselves will be exalted.

(Luke 18:10–14)

Unlike the story of the widow and the unjust judge and, for that matter, unlike every other story from Jesus except his one of the good Samaritan, this parable is precisely located: in the temple at Jerusalem. When he himself went up to pray there, did Jesus himself once observe two men behaving like those in the story of the Pharisee and the tax collector? The vivid, true-to-life quality of the account could easily lead one to think so. This parable may open a window on the world Jesus had seen. Jesus is certainly remembered as noticing what happened in the temple. He singled out for special praise a widow putting her small but most generous contribution into the temple treasury

(Mark 12:41–4). The Gospels all report his outrage at the trading which he saw going on in the temple precincts; he angrily drove out those who defiled the holy place by their business transactions. People and things caught his eye in the temple and its precincts. Perhaps he once overheard two men at prayer there, and his story grew naturally out of that experience. At all events, as in the case of the good Samaritan, Jesus does something startling. He turns for the hero of his story to someone who is far from well regarded: one of the widely disliked tax collectors.

The way the Gospels use the stock phrase 'tax collectors and sinners' (for instance, Matthew 9:10) alerts us to the common contempt in which this profession was held. As they collaborated with the authorities of the Roman Empire, tax collectors were considered disloyal traitors. Since they made their margin of profit by extorting more than was legally due, they were hated for exploiting others. To say the least, Jesus had nerves of steel in proposing as an ideal not the professionally religious Pharisee but a social outcast who followed a despised trade.

It is this outcast who serves to exemplify the right quality of prayer. One should pray not only with the perseverance of the widow demanding justice from the lazy judge, but also with the self-effacement of the tax collector.

THE PHARISEE

The Pharisee has vested interests in the inferiority of others. Even (or should one say especially?) when praying to God, he fosters a sense of his own personal worth by comparing himself to others. He needs to compare himself if he is to sustain his misguided self-image. His feeling of self-reliance and self-assurance expresses itself right from the start: he stands, not with others, but 'by himself' to pray. He then prays in a thoroughly self-serving and self-congratulatory way. Even though he does pray, he never gets around to admitting that he needs anything – even from God. He first formulates his merits negatively: he is 'not like other people'. One can hear the sneer when he dismisses them as being thieves, rogues, adulterers or tax collectors. He has neither fallen into such sins nor kept such bad company. Positively speaking, he has paid to the priests even more than the required tithes, a tenth of his whole income, and gone beyond what the law requires by fasting twice a week. He boasts to God as he catalogues his own virtuous actions. When living his day-to-day existence, the Pharisee keeps a tight control over everything. When praying, he judges and justifies himself.

For good or ill, we all bring ourselves to prayer and pray as the people we are. The Pharisee takes life at all levels to be a matter of one's performance and achievements. His self-confident activity *must* make him acceptable to God. In life's competition, in both material and spiritual matters, the Pharisee has come out on top. He has won; those 'others' have lost out. It is in that spirit that he presents himself to God.

Flannery O'Connor (1925–64), whether she realized it or not, pictured a marvellous counterpart to the Pharisee in the person of Ruby Turpin, the central figure in a short story ('Revelation') that opens in a doctor's waiting room. When she enters, Ruby orders her limping husband to take the only place available. The vast woman stands there, literally towering over everyone else. 'A respectable, hard-working, church-going woman', she knows that one day she will wear a heavenly crown:

'If it's one thing I am,' Mrs. Turpin said with feeling, 'it's grateful. When I think who all I could have been besides myself and what all I got, a little of everything and a good disposition besides, I just feel like shouting, "Thank you, Jesus, for making everything the way it is! It could have been different!"'

She is so glad that she is not 'a nigger or white trash' or any of those other people whom she finds to be unintelligent, dirty and lacking the common sense, social status and good disposition with which she considers herself and her husband to be blessed.

Her self-congratulatory chatter goads into violence another patient waiting to see the doctor. A 'fat girl of eighteen or nineteen' called Mary Grace can no longer stand it when Ruby Turpin cries out, 'Oh thank you, Jesus, Jesus thank you.' She throws a book (significantly entitled *Human Development*) at her, and then jumps on Ruby, telling her: 'Go back to hell where you came from, you old wart hog.' It is a harsh awakening for the self-righteous Ruby. The attack shakes her belief in herself as a Christian woman. She begins to realize that her supposed virtues are meaningless and that she is more a wart hog than a respectable lady.

At the end of the story Ruby is down at the pig-pen on her own farm. She gazes at the grunting, rooting and groaning pigs, and then lifts her eyes up into the sky as the sun is setting. She sees 'a vast horde of people ... rumbling towards heaven', with the 'white trash ... niggers ... and battalions of freaks and lunatics' leading the way. The 'respectable' people are marching a long way behind. Ruby surrenders her self-proclaimed virtues and aligns herself with the vision of those 'climbing upward into the starry field and shouting hallelujah'.

What a pity that there was no Mary Grace around in the temple to shout at the Pharisee: 'Go back to hell where you came from, you old wart hog.' He might have given up his orderly world in which he kept everything tidily under control and admired his own virtuous actions, but failed to see how desperately he too needed God's merciful help.

Jesus himself might have thrown a couple of his parables at the Pharisee. He could have tested him in the light of the story of the unforgiving servant. After all, the Pharisee says not a word about his record in being merciful and forgiving to those who have offended him or owe him something. Is he harsh and lacking in compassion with others? Then how will he show up when tested by the parable of the good Samaritan? Has the Pharisee been proving himself a real neighbour to those in drastic need of his help? Has he been self-giving and not merely self-affirming?

THE TAX COLLECTOR

When we pass from the Pharisee's stream of consciousness to the prayer of the tax collector, we meet someone who confesses that he has nothing to parade before God. He stands 'far off' and 'beats his breast', recognizing with pain and sorrow his own sinfulness: 'God, be merciful to me, a sinner!' By repeatedly imploring the divine mercy, the tax collector finds acceptance from God; things are 'right' between him and God.

A paid-up member of a kind of first-century Mafia organization, the tax collector would never dream of indulging judgemental attitudes towards others. He himself is one of those 'thieves and rogues' that the Pharisee despises. He is miles away from the smug, racist self-satisfaction of Ruby Turpin. He knows that what counts, first and last, is all that God does for us, not what we think we are doing for God. What is decisive is the here and now, our present relationship with God. We are not called to run up an excellent record, on which we can then congratulate ourselves. What we are called to acknowledge, above all in prayer, is our constant need of the divine mercy. This makes me treasure in the Roman Catholic eucharistic service the triple cry for mercy that must never be omitted: 'Lord, have mercy. Christ, have mercy. Lord, have mercy.' Other Christians use this triple appeal in their worship. As nothing else does, it underlines the need of all Christians and, really, of all human beings for the divine mercy.

One startling difference between the Pharisee and the tax collector emerges over the matter of gratitude. To echo the dying man in Bernanos' *Diary of a Country Priest*, 'All is gift and all is grace.' Thanksgiving towards God must shape our lives. At the same time, we can even corrupt this basic duty and introduce unworthy reasons for gratitude. The Pharisee may begin by saying, 'God, I thank you,' but at once the prayer heads in a self-centred direction. He does not pray: 'O God, I thank you for being what you are, the utterly wonderful God of the universe. I thank you for your great mercy and loving kindness towards all of us. I thank you for the particular kindness and goodness that I constantly experience from you in my own life.'

It is easy, of course, to criticize the Pharisee over this and other points. But where is gratitude and thanksgiving in the prayer of the tax collector? How can he, according to Jesus, go home 'justified' and 'exalted', if his prayer is simply 'be merciful to me a sinner'? I hope it is not special pleading to point out that gratitude and thanksgiving are implied in the tax collector's prayer. He calls to mind the prodigal son, who returns home with a very similar prayer to make. The parable of the prodigal son celebrates the mercy of God, who reaches out with unconditional love to all sinners. Those who join in the prayers of the prodigal son and the tax collector acknowledge humbly and gratefully the astounding God to whom they return.

TWO CONCLUDING THOUGHTS

Over the years I have heard many preachers and others remark that there is something of the Pharisee and something of the tax collector in all of us. The thesis is plausible and delivers an open invitation to do what no one else can do for us: examine our own consciences in the light of the parable. Easily the most poignant occasion when I heard such a comment came in late 1989, when I met a young priest who had just arrived from the Jesuit university in San Salvador to study at the Biblical Institute in Rome. We happened to start talking about the parable of the Pharisee and the tax collector. 'You know,' he told me, 'recently we spent a long time talking through that parable in our community. We really wondered whether we were more like the Pharisee – thinking that *we* were living virtuously and not like all those rogues who don't commit themselves to working for the poor and oppressed.' A month or two later, six of his Jesuit friends in that community, along with their cook and the cook's daughter, were savagely gunned down one night by the military. I like to think that, when welcoming them into heaven, Jesus thanked them for taking his parable to heart.

Apropos of Jesus, one cannot miss an ironical aspect to the Pharisee's boast about the company he does *not* keep. The Pharisee does not associate with 'thieves, rogues, adulterers, and tax collectors'. That was exactly the company that Jesus preferred during his ministry. Only a chapter later in Luke's Gospel one reads, for instance, of Jesus' visiting the home of a district tax collector, Zacchaeus (Luke 19:1–10). But his liking for 'bad company' did not stop Jesus from also visiting the homes of Pharisees, as the same Gospel of Luke likes to stress. Jesus associates with everyone; he is the friend of all.

A PRAYER

> O merciful God, take from us all self-serving vanity and self-congratulatory pride.
> Give us the courage to face our sins and our daily need for your compassion.
> Make us cry out constantly, 'Be merciful to me, a sinner.'

EXERCISES

1 If someone were to listen in to your prayer, what would they hear?

2 Many comment on the parable of the prodigal son by saying that there is something of both sons in all of us. Would you agree that, likewise, there is something of the Pharisee and the tax collector in all of us?

PART FOUR

AT THE END

CHAPTER FIFTEEN

THE WEEDS IN THE WHEAT

The kingdom of heaven may be compared to someone who sowed good seed in his field; but while everybody was asleep, an enemy came and sowed weeds among the wheat, and then went away. So when the plants came up and bore grain, then the weeds appeared as well. And the servants of the householder came and said to him, 'Master, did you not sow good seed in your field? Where, then, did these weeds come from?' He answered, 'An enemy has done this.' The servants said to him, 'Then do you want us to go and gather them?' But he replied, 'No; for in gathering the weeds you would uproot the wheat along with them. Let both of them grow together until the harvest; and at harvest time I will tell the reapers; Collect the weeds first and bind them in bundles to be burned, but gather the wheat into my barn.'

(Matthew 13:24–30)

The late Flannery O'Connor, who drew bizarre characters and events to fashion her wonderful insights into the human condition, had no illusions about the world she lived in. She saw reality as territory largely held by the devil. No gloomy pessimist, she opened her sharp eyes to the violent struggle between good and evil going on everywhere. She shared that vision of conflict with her readers, assuring them that at the end 'a vast horde of people' will go 'rumbling towards heaven', 'shouting hallelujah' as they climb upwards.

I don't know whether O'Connor ever read the poetry of
David Gascoyne (b. 1916). She kept writing her novels and
short stories until lupus carried her away at the age of 39, while
Gascoyne spent years struggling for his mental equilibrium. In
his greatest poem, 'Ecce Homo', he contemplates the crucified
Jesus suspended against the murderous history of a world in
which 'fear and greed are sovereign lords'. As much as, or perhaps more than, any other period of recorded history, the twentieth century shows how destructive and even genocidal our
fear and greed can prove. Tragically, so many of these murders
have been committed, as Gascoyne put it, by 'Christian warriors defending faith and property'.

CHRISTIANS AND THEIR LEADERS

It is painful enough to contemplate the apocalyptic evil human
beings have dealt out to each other. It can be even more painful
to recall the ghastly sins of Christians and their leaders. Several
months ago a friend shared with me his unpublished manuscript, which aims to lead people into prayer but also wants to
tackle difficulties that can drive them away from the Church.
This wonderful friend shows breathtaking humility in accepting the tough and, I must confess, harsh criticism that his writing has at times drawn from me. My last letter was, thank God,
a bit milder. Among other things I said:

I do appreciate what you say about people who drift away from
the Church, upset by her social and human failings. Many folk
I know are like that. My hope is like yours: to help them recon-
nect with the living person of Jesus. It does help to remind them
that Jesus' community has been rather wretched right from the
beginning. First Corinthians shows us a group of Christians
who get drunk, are fiercely divided and divisive, have radical
problems about the resurrection, are disorderly in their prayer
services, take each other to court etc. The 'etc.' includes at least

one case of incest and a number of wealthier persons not caring about the poorer Christians. Right from the outset Jesus' chosen friends have proved a rum lot. But if we are going to relate to him (the Bridegroom), we have to relate to his bride, the Church. There is nothing new at all about being scandalized over the conduct of Jesus' community. It's good, I believe, to remind people that there never was a golden age; we in the Church were a desperate lot from the start.

In retrospect, I wonder whether I should have frankly shared with this friend the shame that I at times feel over the conduct of many Christians and their leaders. Did I make things too easy for myself with a bland generalization about 'social and human failings'?

SOCIAL AND HUMAN FAILINGS

Awful weeds show up constantly in the life of the world-wide Church. Death squads justify their murders by calling themselves 'the warriors of Christ the King'. For years I have been haunted by a line from W.H. Auden's 'Spain' ('the conscious acceptance of guilt in the necessary murder'), especially as adapted by Raymond Williams:

It is interesting to imagine the line rewritten as 'the conscious acceptance of guilt in the necessary killing' and then ask how many people, in reality, dissent from this. Most people I know, and most humane liberals I have heard of, accept killing in this sense again and again.[1]

Williams wrote about 'most people' and 'most humane liberals'. But reconsidering his remarks, we might ask ourselves about 'most Christians'. Too many consciously accept the necessary killing, with high-tech weapons, of 'those on the other side', or at least of the military forces of 'those others'. What else is happening but such 'necessary killing' when unborn children are aborted – of course, for the 'best' of reasons? Do Williams' words merit application to churchgoing Christian leaders who support partial birth abortions, which involve children's skulls being first crushed and then sucked out?

What I facilely called 'social and human failings' include paedophilia committed against the young and defenceless by clergy and other religious. They also cover shady financial dealings in which church leaders may indulge, and occasions when some bishops quarrel over their cut from a huge bequest. Sexual and financial sins belong among the terrible weeds to which journalists constantly and rightly alert the general public.

The media often reacts also to those Christians who make a virtue out of tearing down or reducing basic beliefs and practices they have inherited. Without indulging in self-dramatization, I have to admit being grieved every now and then to read of some Christian teachers and leaders who busy themselves telling the public what central doctrines do not mean. At times they seem to want to spend time parodying and then ridiculing basic beliefs, rather than doing something much harder: exploring ways of bringing out the meaning and vital significance of central articles of our faith.

Years ago I met two teachers responsible for Christian doctrine in a number of primary schools. They boasted of a method which they had developed to stop little boys and girls from attributing products directly to God: 'We pull out of our pocket an orange, put it on the desk and ask: "Who made that?" Naturally the children say, "God made the orange." We keep repeating our question until they come to realize and say that oranges come from orange trees and not from God.'

It grieved me then and grieves me now that Christian doctrine classes could have been misused to diminish little boys' and girls' spontaneous insights into God's power and presence. Children obviously cannot be expected to distinguish between God (the primary Cause of everything) and other, secondary, causes. But in their own way they know that oranges are made both by God and by orange trees. Teachers who feel some moral necessity to get rid of religious convictions are lining themselves up with the weeds rather than the wheat.

Such reductionist habits in matters of doctrine often coincide with and complement similar habits in the area of morals. Ethical principles can be shed or changed when they are found to be 'inconvenient'. Moral reductionism at times seems to go so scandalously far as to drop all principles except a vague compassion.

In his manuscript, my friend wrote about 'the Church persecuting those with prophetic insight'. I commented on this criticism as being 'unqualified' and added: 'Do you mean some officials with power, not the Church as such?' Nevertheless, my friend touched a neuralgic point. Recently another, much older friend of mine found his latest book being dishonestly reviewed in a leading church paper. Subsequently his work was incriminated at two official meetings that he knew nothing about until months later. Rather than any difficulties with his writings being given an open and clearly Christian hearing, the events smacked of totalitarian practice: first the smear and then a secret trial leading to a kind of academic lynching. My language may be excessive and too strong. But can I rebut those who read off such events that way? Or those who call attention to many ways in which sexism, racialism, nationalism, careerism and other 'isms' taint the life of the Church?

WHEAT AS WELL AS WEEDS

When we look at the 'field', we will probably be like the servants in the parable who do not tell the householder: 'The good seed is coming up nicely. But we have also spotted a fair number of weeds growing up as well.' No, they bolt straight to the question: 'Where did these weeds come from?'[2] Jesus catches something that seems universally true. It is so much easier to notice what is going wrong than what is going right. An old adage tells us: 'Good from something complete, evil from any defect at all (*bonum ex integra causa, malum ex quocumque defectu*)'. Unless something is perfect and is working perfectly, our eye will automatically pick up a defect, which may after all be only minor.

Good grain abounds in our Church and our world. In the unpublished manuscript of my younger friend I remarked how he persistently used 'institutional' as a negative adjective, and wrote:

Now what's wrong with institutions in general? The alternative is a world of anarchy and chaos ... Sociologists, or at least some of them I have read, have shown me how institutions like parishes can aid people in their religious and human growth. In Rome some of the people I admire most are the clergy who battle away in the working–class areas, trying to help people of all ages and often in the face of huge difficulties. A short time ago a parish priest had petrol poured over him and was set on fire, while he was praying one morning before Mass. His crime? Trying to help young people kick the drug habit. To be sure, institutions can be unhealthy, corrupt and the rest, but so can families and human beings in general.

From the beginning the Church has been a messy institution, in which we can always find plenty of sins, tensions and mistaken ideas. But, like a good 'householder', Jesus wants us to see the grain and not spend all our time moaning over the terrible weeds. The routine denigration of failures and scandals in Christianity can overlook the millions of men and women who, regularly in the face of great difficulties, offer shining examples of what following Jesus entails as we wait for the full coming of his kingdom.

With his picture of a field of wheat mixed with weeds, Jesus obviously encourages us to endure with patience this less than perfect situation. He certainly does not ask us to approve of the weeds, let alone encourage their growth. But he does ask us to show forbearance and not lash out angrily. The present situation of the Church and the world is certainly not all that it should be. But God's final judgement is coming and will vindicate what is right. There will be no weeds in the final kingdom. But until that comes, we must endure their persistent presence.

A Prayer

> O gracious God, your Son has not called us to be softly tolerant of evil.
> But he does invite us to endure with patience the evils in our world and Church.
> Give us the strength to bear with all that we may deplore but cannot change,
> knowing that in your final kingdom all things shall be well.

Exercises

1 What are the 'weeds' that trouble you most in the life of the Church?
2 Does it help you to remember that, right from the start, Christian communities suffered from serious problems and failings?
3 How does the parable of the weeds in the wheat converge with and differ from that of the dragnet (Matthew 13:47–52)?

1 R. Williams, *Modern Tragedy* (London: Chatto & Windus, 1966), p. 195, n. 1.
2 Nowadays the farm workers would think of some nasty saboteur tampering with the bags coming from the grain silo, and would probably suggest spraying the crop with weed killer. The owner would tell them to let the harvester do its work in sorting the wheat from the weeds when it goes through the fields.

CHAPTER SIXTEEN

THE WATCHFUL SERVANTS

Be dressed for action and have your lamps lit; be like those who are waiting for their master to return from the wedding banquet, so that they may open the door to him as soon as he comes and knocks. Blessed are those servants whom the master finds awake when he comes; truly I tell you, he will fasten his belt and have them sit down to eat; and he will come and serve them. If he comes in the middle of the night, or near dawn, and finds them so, blessed are those servants.

(Luke 12:35–8)

Several of Jesus' parables underline the need for his followers to show vigilance and faithfulness as they wait for the end. Here he does so by pulling in the image of a great household and its master who is out for the night. Undoubtedly Jesus had first heard of and then seen for himself such households. Did he know people who worked in such households, or had he even himself worked at times for such households? During his ministry we find Jesus a guest of some wealthy householders (for instance, Luke 7:36–50; 19:1–10). Whether or not he enjoyed many personal connections with such great households, they caught his imagination and provided material for some of his parables.

SERVANTS AND BRIDESMAIDS

The parable we look at first in this chapter resembles somewhat that of the wise and foolish bridesmaids (Matthew 25:1–13). Both stories feature a wedding, people waiting for a central figure who is currently absent but certain to arrive, and the need for lamps to be kept alight. Both stories turn on the fact that the precise time of the arrival – in the first case, of the bridegroom, and in the second, of the master – is not known in advance. They could turn up at any time; no one knows exactly when. But then the differences between the two stories set in. The story from Matthew specifies a particular number of young women, ten bridesmaids, while our parable from Luke includes an indefinite number of servants, who include men and women. These servants are expected to stay awake and not fall asleep, as *all* the bridesmaids do. In that other story the wise bridesmaids doze off along with the foolish ones; their advantage consists not in staying awake but in having a good supply of oil, which the others lack.

Further, Matthew's story initially stations all the bridesmaids outside; they are meant to join the procession when the bridegroom fetches his bride from her parents' home. Five of the bridesmaids fail to make the rendezvous and take part in the procession. They have slipped away to buy some oil from dealers (who apparently keep long trading hours). Hence they turn up late and are not admitted when they knock on the door of the bridegroom's house. In Luke's parable, however, the servants are all inside, and should be ready at any moment to open the door and serve a meal. They are waiting for their master to come home from a wedding banquet, not for a bridegroom himself. It is the master himself who will arrive back when he wants to and will knock at the door of his own house, not five foolish bridesmaids who knock at someone else's door when they arrive too late.

THE MASTER AS SERVANT

In Luke's story of the servants waiting at home, they are expected to carry out their normal duties. They are not given extraordinary commissions like the three servants in the parable of the talents who receive very large amounts of money for trading or at least investment purposes. The expectations are the customary ones when their master is away briefly – perhaps only out for the night – at a banquet. Up and dressed for action, his servants should keep their lamps lit and have food ready for their master when he returns. The last item seems puzzling. Hasn't he been at a banquet? In that Mediterranean culture it would have been considered shameful not to feed guests very well, in fact to overfeed them. Why would the master want to eat? Surely his first thought on returning at midnight or towards dawn would be to head for bed and enjoy some good hours of sleep? Or perhaps we are to suppose that the wedding and the subsequent banquet took place at some distance – a day's journey away. But this puzzle pales into insignificance when we read on.

If the servants have been vigilantly ready for the master's return, he will turn around and, even though it is late at night, will offer them a meal at which he himself will serve at table. In an amazing reversal of roles, this wealthy master will not only put on a banquet for his staff but also will take over the job of waiter. Any thought is forgotten of his being tired when he returns late at night from the wedding to which he was invited.

This astonishing conclusion to the parable brings two things to mind. First, the story Jesus tells here inevitably makes us think of another night scene involving a master and his servants. John's Gospel describes Jesus himself doing something similar but even more startling on his last evening with his core group of disciples. He gets up from the supper table, takes off his outer garment, ties a towel around his waist, and washes the feet of his friends (John 13:2–17). John presents that action not so much as a reward for faithful vigilance, but as a stunning example of loving service. Jesus wants to encourage his disciples to imitate humble service of love: 'If I, your Lord and Teacher, have washed your feet, you also ought to wash one another's feet. For I have set you an example, that you also should do as I have done to you.' Jesus' action and intention differ from that of the master in the parable. But there is a similar astounding switch of roles between the divine Lord and his followers.

Second, the parable of the watchful servants ends with a surprise meal for them – a closing detail that summons up the final banquet for all in the coming kingdom of God, a theme which surfaces here and there in Jesus' preaching and teaching (for instance, Luke 13:29; 22:16) and not least in the story of the prodigal son (see Chapters 2 and 3 above). The father holds a feast of joy and thanksgiving to celebrate the new life at which his sinful younger son has arrived.

In the 'Our Father' we pray 'your kingdom come', but we might also be more specific: 'May the banquet of your kingdom come.' The master's late-night banquet for all his vigilant servants directs our gaze forward – to what is to come in the glorious completion of God's reign. The best is yet to come. The main perspective is undoubtedly the final revelation of the glorious Christ and the shape of things to come for everybody at the end of all history. Nevertheless, this frame of mind does not exclude post-death expectations for the individual. In fact, Luke encourages his readers to include that perspective by attaching to the story of the watchful servants two further passages which encourage watchfulness, but which do so by appealing to two *individual* figures: an owner of the house alert to the possibility of burglary, and a 'faithful and prudent manager'.

THE WATCHFUL HOUSEHOLDER

Luke reports Jesus' words on the watchful householder:

But know this: if the owner of the house had known at what hour
the thief was coming, he would not have let his house be broken
into. You also must be ready, for the Son of Man is coming at an
unexpected hour.

(Luke 12:39–40)

Here, obviously, the warning has nothing to do with a delay in a
robber's arrival. In the story of the watchful servants, as in the
case of the wise and foolish bridesmaids, someone is absent but
will certainly turn up, even if his arrival may be considerably
delayed. In the case of the watchful householder, word has got
around about burglaries taking place in the neighbourhood. Are
we to imagine a situation that can occur today in a large town?
All the other houses on the street have been 'done'. When will
they come to break into mine? Yet no one can be certain that the
prowling robbers will try to break into every house in the vicin-
ity, even less into this particular one.[1] Even if a householder
were certain that they would try to break in, because – let us say
– robbers have already hit every other house in the village and
they have a reputation for being 'thorough', he still would not
know the day, let alone the hour, when the robbers would
arrive. A wise householder must be constantly watchful in
guarding his house against a possible break-in. He should also
keep in mind that smart burglars may very well come right at a
time when we don't expect them.

This kind of language might encourage us to create the title
for Jesus 'the Smart Burglar', rather than stick with the traditional phrase of 'a thief in the night' (1 Thessalonians 5:2).
Whatever we prefer, Jesus warns us that his coming will be unexpected. It will be unexpected when he comes to end human
history and complete the glorious reign of God. It is persistently
unexpected when he comes at the end of individual lives.
Occasionally relatives and friends can anticipate that some very
sick person will slip away to God today or tomorrow. Yet even
with those who are obviously dying the precise timing of death

very often has something surprising about it. Quite regularly we have to say, 'The Son of Man came at an unexpected hour.'

Recently a friend of mine who has cared for many dying people told me how rarely he could predict when death would happen. Milton could talk with someone, leave for other appointments, and learn later that the patient had died twenty or thirty minutes after he left.

THE FAITHFUL MANAGER

Luke links yet another story to the parable of the watchful servants: that of a trusty and sensible manager:

The Lord said, 'Who then is the faithful and prudent manager whom his master will put in charge of his servants, to give them their allowance of food at the proper time? Blessed is that servant whom his master will find at work when he arrives. Truly I tell you, he will put that one in charge of all his possessions. But if that servant says to himself, 'My master is delayed in coming,' and if he begins to beat the other servants, men and women, and to eat and drink and get drunk, the master of that servant will come on a day when he does not expect him and at an hour that he does not know, and will cut him to pieces, and put him with the unfaithful.

(Luke 12:42–6)

With this story we leave the image of a householder and return to that of servants or even slaves. But this time Jesus does not look at these domestics as a group who must be dressed for action and about their duties. He focuses rather on an individual, a manager whom the master has put in charge while he goes off somewhere for some unspecified purpose and also for an unspecified amount of time. This individual, so far from receiving such a dramatic responsibility as that of investing bags of gold for his absent master, is simply expected to carry out the ordinary duties of providing a regular amount of food for the other servants at the usual times.

But the consequences for the manager are startling. If he behaves in a faithful and sensible way, he will receive a remarkable promotion: he will be put in charge of all the master's possessions. But if he has abused his power and proved arrogant, he will be 'cut to pieces' and 'put with the unfaithful'. One flinches at these words which conclude the parable. With this threat of being torn asunder, we seem to stare into the face of irrational cruelty. Some scholars interpret being 'cut to pieces' as being 'punished severely'. Even so, being then 'put with the unfaithful' may seem excessive. Why not simply demote the unfaithful manager, keep him within the establishment, and have him do penance for his irresponsible behaviour? Surely he could be ordered to serve time by working with the lowest rank of servants or even with the slaves?

The alternatives Jesus proposes are stark – either being put in charge of everything or being 'cut to pieces'. But he certainly wants to underline the need for vigilant and serious fidelity as our end draws near. The parable of the watchful servants describes the amazing and unexpected generosity of the master who finds his servants waiting for him when he returns from a wedding. These servants will be blessed in a remarkable fashion. But what if they fail to wait up and keep their lamps lit? The parable with which we began this chapter does not spell out the consequences of such a failure. As Luke the Evangelist realized, the story of the watchful servants needs to be filled out by the story of the watchful householder and that of the faithful manager. The latter story more than hints at life in the early Christian communities – and, for that matter, Christian communities today. The responsibilities of those called to exercise leadership roles in the household of God are awesome and daunting.

All three parables inculcate the call to vigilant responsibility, reaching a crescendo with the third. Names play their role in producing this crescendo of seriousness. The watchful servants wait for 'their master' (*kurios*) to return. The second parable, that of the watchful householder, emphasizes the disciples' need to be always ready for the unpredictable and unexpected coming of the Son of Man, who will bring the final reign of God. Luke puts the third parable in the mouth of 'the Lord (*ho Kurios*)', who indicates how he will arrive to judge his servants and followers for their fidelity or infidelity. We are dealing with the one life and death we face, matters of vital importance. The crucial issue of our fate demands these three utterly serious parables from Jesus.

A Prayer

> O Lord, support us all the day long,
> until the shadows lengthen and the evening comes,
> and the busy world is hushed, and the fever of life is over,
> and our work is done.
> Then in thy mercy grant us a safe lodging, and a holy rest,
> and peace at the last.

Exercises

1 Could you compose a modern version of the parable of the watchful servants by using those employed in a large firm and imagining what happens when their managing director returns after being away for some time?

2 Recall some personal experiences of deaths which came as 'a thief in the night'.

3 Compare and contrast the parable of the watchful servants with that of the servant's reward (Luke 17:7–10).

1 Nowadays Jesus could have drawn a story from the firemen working at a large airport. They keep their fire engines constantly ready. Everyone hopes that they will never have to deal with a crash; in fact, for decades an airport can remain free from any accidents. But one never knows; some firemen must be vigilantly prepared to cope with an emergency that might never happen.

CHAPTER SEVENTEEN

THE RICH FOOL

The land of a rich man produced abundantly. And he thought to himself, 'What should I do, for I have no place to store my crops?' Then he said, 'I will do this: I will pull down my barns and build larger ones, and there I will store all my grain and my goods. And I will say to my soul, "Soul, you have ample goods laid up for many years; relax, eat, drink, be merry." ' But God said to him, 'You fool! This very night your life is demanded of you. And the things you have prepared, whose will they be?' So it is with those who store up treasures for themselves but are not rich towards God.

(Luke 12:16–21)

Where the parable of the watchful servants encouraged and illustrated the expectation of the Lord's coming appropriately shared by the community, with the story of the rich fool the focus shifts to an individual. The reader overhears the rich man's soliloquy, when he thinks 'to himself' and speaks 'to his soul'. The situation changes abruptly when God speaks to him. Instead of enjoying 'many years' of comfortable living and cheerful feasting, the rich man must face death that very night. He has been mistaken in the way he presumes to control his life and prepare his future: building larger barns and storing up all his goods will not guarantee his lasting future. Others will inherit his property and he himself will go empty-handed to meet God.

The story gives no hint that this rich man has gained his wealth through illegal activities. He is not to be compared with modern tycoons whose dishonest dealings can yield incredible results. Slumps in the market may destroy their opulent lifestyle, and their financial failure often brings ruin to many others. In the parable of the rich fool the man has become very affluent through the fertility of his land: God has blessed him with abundant harvests. The death of the rich man will not ruin anyone. Others, one presumes members of his family, will inherit all this possessions.

What has gone wrong, then? The rich man has failed to recognize that he holds his life and wealth on loan from God. It does not occur to him to praise and thank God for all the abundant blessings he has received. Rather, he sets about planning a future in a completely self-sufficient way: 'I will do this; I will pull down my barns and build larger ones, and there I will store all my grain and my goods.' He deludes himself into imagining that he can organize and expect an affluent existence 'for many years'. It takes only a sudden heart attack or cerebral haemorrhage to put an abrupt end to his self-centred plans for opulent living.

The parable inevitably recalls that of the rich man and Lazarus. In both cases, we hear the voice of some heavenly figure delivering a warning about the need to repent in time. Yet we should not miss the difference. In that other story it is Abraham who speaks, even if one must admit that he does so with divine authority and is in a position to share divine blessings. Being at Abraham's side in the other world brings Lazarus nothing less than the happiness of heaven. Nevertheless, in the story of the rich fool the solemn warning comes when God himself speaks to the rich man, and God's word of warning will certainly be fulfilled. That man will not live to enjoy another day; he will die during the night.

In the parable of the rich man and Lazarus two people die, the poor man dying (perhaps of hunger) before the rich, well-fed one. But, after sketching the scene of feasting and famine, the story makes no particular issue of how soon death comes to either of them. The timing of death, however, essentially shapes the story of the rich fool. The rich landowner plans 'many years' of comfortable living, but death comes for him the very night he makes those plans. A dramatic contrast is drawn between his long-term plans and their abrupt frustration.

The two stories also move apart somewhat by variations in religious directness. The parable of the rich man and Lazarus tells of angels caring for the poor man after death, locates its second act in heaven and hell, engages Abraham in dialogue with the rich man, refers to Moses and the prophets, and alludes to the climax of divine revelation and salvation: Jesus' being raised from the dead. Nevertheless, this parable does not directly name God, still less put God on the stage. Here the story of the rich fool strikingly differs. Its denouement comes when God speaks – the only time God ever speaks in any of Jesus' parables. The story ends with the call to be 'rich towards God'. Human destiny depends upon one's relationship to God.

JESUS ON DEATH

The theme of a sudden death shapes the parable of the rich fool. How did this theme enter into the preaching of Jesus? Jesus knew as well as anyone that death will submerge every earthly task and plan – whether sacred or secular. But he faced the whole of life without a trace of morbid contempt, and disdained nothing for being transient. As we have repeatedly seen in the earlier chapters, the whole span of human experience mattered to him: a boy who takes his money and leaves home; day-labourers harvesting grapes; farmers trudging up and down as they sow their crops; women mixing yeast in the dough; widows failing to secure justice from the courts; travellers at risk from bandits. Jesus ignored and discarded nobody and nothing. He brought his good news of the kingdom to bear on all that people around him were doing. He assured his audience that nothing of our human reality lacks worth and value in the sight of God: 'Even the hairs of your head are all counted' (Luke 12:7).

Jesus never urged his hearers to detach themselves from the worthless things of the body, or to seek release from the ills of earthly existence. In fact, he worked miracles that restored people to complete bodily integrity. Those who were cured could see again, walk erect, cook meals, and live once more with their families in a normal human fashion. Sickness or physical handicaps had cut them off from the full range of normal activities. In the case of lepers, their disease had excluded them from living in cities or villages with other men and women. By healing the sick Jesus reinserted them into human society. His miraculous deeds resulted in a wholesome rehumanization. He enabled the sick and handicapped to enjoy once again complete bodily welfare as healthy men and women.

All of this contrasts sharply with the attitude of Socrates, as it is affectionately described in the *Phaedo*. He sees true life as entailing nothing less than a strict preparation for death. The philosopher rehearses dying, longs to escape from imprisonment by the body, and welcomes death as the gateway to the true, spiritual world. As he waits for the gaoler to bring him the hemlock, Socrates explains to his friends why 'a man who has really spent his life in philosophy is naturally glad when he is on the point of dying':

Those who apply themselves correctly to the pursuit of philosophy are in fact practising nothing more nor less than dying and death. If this is so, it would indeed be strange that men who throughout their lives sought precisely this, should grumble when it came – the very thing which they had, for so long, desired and rehearsed.[1]

Jesus, however, taught people to practise living, not rehearse dying. Even if the language may not derive directly from the earthly Jesus, some words in the Fourth Gospel catch nicely the thrust of Jesus' ministry: 'I came that they may have life, and have it abundantly' (John 10:10). Jesus never said and, frankly, I can never imagine him saying: 'I came that they may practise death, and rehearse it more seriously.' When he himself reached 'the point of dying', he cried out against it in the garden of Gethsemane rather than showing himself 'naturally glad'. He never urged his hearers: 'Emancipate yourselves from the bondage of flesh by discipline, detachment and prayer. Life after death is the only true reality.'

The preaching of Jesus, while introducing death in the two forceful parables of the rich man and Lazarus and that of the rich fool, did not morbidly dwell on the topic. We would misrepresent the ministry of Jesus if we summed it all up as a cry: 'Prepare for death!' Instead, in his own unique way Jesus pushed at people the message: 'Practise true life!' He was no Platonist, anxious to shed the body, set the soul free and get away to the real world. Jesus could never accept the moral that Sigmund Freud drew from *King Lear* – that we should 'renounce life and renounce love and make friends with the necessity of dying'.

Christian asceticism has included a hardy tradition which represents life as a persistent 'preparation for death (*preparatio mortis*)'. *The Imitation of Christ* by Thomas à Kempis (ca. 1380–1471) warns us: 'You ought so to order yourself in all your thoughts and actions, as if today you were to die' (1.23). We hear similar advice from the baroque German poetry of Angelus Silesius (1624–77): 'Because through death alone we become liberated, I say it is the best of all things created.'[2] Books on 'the art of dying (*ars moriendi*)' enjoyed great popularity in the late Middle Ages. This literature expressed and reinforced the portrayals of death in art. European cemeteries often featured the 'Dance of Death'. In these compositions death, normally represented as a skeleton, led men and women, depicted in various conditions and states of life, in a dance towards the grave. Visitors to the church of Santa Maria Novella in Florence will not easily forget the words at the foot of Masaccio's masterly portrayal of the crucifixion. A skeleton tells the viewer: 'What you are I once was. What I am you one day will be.'

In a scene from his *Portrait of the Artist as a Young Man* (1916), James Joyce brilliantly records the terror preachers could arouse by talking about death and what follows. I remember hearing such sermons and reading such literature in my own youth. One story which sticks in my mind came from Paolo Segneri (1624–94), a vivid and popular Italian preacher. He pictured an aristocrat lying on his death-bed – flanked, on the one side, by his mistress and, on the other, by a priest holding a crucifix. Would the dying man give his last kiss to his mistress or to Christ? I recall a nurse in my home city of Melbourne, who amused herself by attending missions preached in parish churches. She used to compare and contrast various stories of deaths, sudden and otherwise, that the wandering preachers invoked to encourage repentance and conversion.

Now set the Sermon on the Mount (Matthew 5–7) alongside all these ascetical warnings. Jesus yields to no one in his ultimate seriousness. But, so far from calling for the constant contemplation of death, he invites us to seek 'God's kingdom and its righteousness', refrain from being 'anxious about tomorrow', and realize that today has enough troubles of its own (Matthew 6:33–4). Jesus wants us to think upon his words and put them into practice (Matthew 7:24–7), not to brood endlessly upon death. Jesus is too busy speaking of life to lapse into any sombre obsession with mortality. His Sermon on the Mount gathers up a generous armful of human experiences: the sight of a hilltop town, quarrels between brothers, the administration of the law, men lusting after other men's wives, houses ransacked by thieves, buildings demolished by floods.

But Jesus never stops to evoke that common experience which *The Imitation of Christ* recalls: 'If at any time you have seen another man die, realize that you must also pass the same way' (1.23).

It is, of course, ultimate folly to forget our mortality. In some parts of today's world human life expectation is ever so much longer than it was in the days of Thomas à Kempis, Masaccio, Angelus Silesius and Paolo Segneri. Many people succumb to the temptation to ignore or even deny death. The parable of the rich fool recalls our common destiny, death; we are foolish if we dismiss it from our mind and thoughts. But this parable gives remembering death (the *memento mori*) a special twist. We have life on loan from God. Both here and hereafter, our existence comes from God and is owed to God.

A Prayer

> Lord God, protector of those who hope in you,
> without whom nothing is strong, nothing holy,
> support us always with your love.
> Guide us so to use the good things of this world,
> that even now we may hold fast to what endures for ever.

Exercises

1 In the Book of Job a very rich man loses his wealth and his health. But how does the story of Job differ from that of the rich fool?

2 What modern parallels do you find to the parable of the rich fool?

3 Try writing your own obituary. If that is too difficult, try writing the obituary of someone very dear to you.

1 Plato, *Phaedo*, 63E–64A, trans. R.S. Bluck (London: Routledge & Kegan Paul, 1955). pp. 46–7.

2 *The Cherubinic Wanderer*, trans. M. Shrady, The Classics of Western Spirituality (New York: Paulist Press, 1986), p. 41. Even more striking is Angelus Silesius' epigram 107 from Book 4, which was not selected for this edition: 'Think upon death, Christian. Why think of the rest? There is nothing more profitable one can think upon than the manner in which we should die' (trans. my own).

Epilogue

Walter's home is thirty miles from Rome, at the southern end of the Alban Hills in a valley outside Velletri. It is a green and fertile zone, under the shadow of an extinct volcano. He lives there with his wife, his son and daughter, his crippled brother and his widowed mother. The garden generously yields peas, beans, broccoli, artichokes and other vegetables. In late spring the apricots ripen, followed by the peaches. In the autumn apples and pears hang on the trees. Above the garden a chicken coop fits into the slope of the mountain. Inside the solid, two-storey country house, a large fire welcomes you into the living room. I sat there last winter to smell the scent of burning wood and talk with Walter about Jesus' parables.

The only Italian I know with the name of Walter, my friend runs a small building company and loves to talk about matters theological and ecclesiastical. On that winter's day he concluded his discourse about the parables by saying: 'God is simple and we are complicated.' Walter was on target, I felt, and I told him that he had another Italian on his side, St Thomas Aquinas. Born and raised only a few miles further south, Aquinas cherished the simplicity of God. The parables more than hint at Jesus' personal identity. They are divinely simple and, one might add, simply divine. Let me explain.

St Gregory the Great (ca. 540–604), in an often quoted comment, remarked that the scriptures provide water in which lambs may gambol and elephants swim. What holds true of the Bible in general proves true also of Jesus' parables in particular. They are not only lively and readable but also endlessly meaningful and inexhaustibly enriching. No reader, not even the holiest and most intelligent reader, can ever dare say: 'Now I understand these parables, and can sum up their meaning once and for all.' The more we explore, the more remains to be explored. Bringing as they do a living encounter with Jesus, they enable everyone to glimpse the mysterious depth of his mind and heart. Far from being open to an adequate interpretation in 'objective', 'scientific' language, the parables invite us to be drawn into the narrative and to share in Jesus' vision of reality. How did he see human life? What did he expect from us? The parables enable us to struggle with these questions, and to do so for a lifetime without ever producing definitive answers. We can only pray: 'May we be made worthy of the divine mercy revealed and embodied in Jesus – not least as the teller of these remarkable stories.'

Admittedly, Jesus had much more to say and to do than tell his stories. At our peril we reduce him to being a 'mere' story-teller who offered spiritual direction through his parables. In any case, as we have repeatedly seen, Jesus dramatized the parables in the events of his own life, death and resurrection. The story-teller personified the story. In that story Jesus overcame death and reconciled us to God. We can stake our lives on Jesus, who showed himself to be not only the Spiritual Director but also the Saviour of the world.

Before closing this book, let me add a few words of summary and explanation. Looking back at the twenty-four parables we have examined, we might classify them in various ways. First, they involve different numbers of characters. Only one woman searches for the lost coin and only one merchant goes in search of the pearl of great value. Two men go up to the temple in the parable of the Pharisee and the tax collector. Three servants receive large sums of money in the parable of the talents. The labourers in the vineyard and the watchful servants feature unspecified numbers of protagonists. Second, some of the characters speak, like the two sons in the parable of the prodigal son. Others remain silent, like the labourers who begin work in the vineyard at five o'clock. Third, we find some persons at home (for instance, a woman in the story of the hidden yeast), others in some work place (for instance, in the labourers in the vineyard), others again travelling (for instance, in the good Samaritan), and yet others again at prayer (the only case being the Pharisee and the tax collector). Fourth, some parables present people behaving well (for instance, in the story of the watchful servants); others present people behaving badly (for instance, in the story of the unforgiving servant). Some parables, such as that of the widow and the unjust judge, portray both good and bad behaviour.

In Chapter 5 I pointed to the wide range of human experiences on which Jesus drew for his parables and to certain common experiences which do not turn up in these stories. We might now add some further items to the list of Jesus' 'silences'. He healed many sick persons, but no parable, with the exception of the rich man and Lazarus and the good Samaritan, brings in someone's infirmity. Otherwise all the characters in the parables seem remarkably healthy, and even energetic. Second, while Jesus introduced death in at least two parables, he never talks of anyone's birth and childhood. Some exquisite passages in the scriptures which he inherited celebrate the birth of some very significant and royal child: for instance, Isaiah 7:10–17; 9:2–7, and 11:1–9. But – is it because of his sensitive delicacy? – Jesus does not bring conception and birth into his stories. He offers a parable on children in the marketplace (Matthew 11:16–19). But normally his parables, while they picture adults doing various things, never introduce the begetting and raising of children.

Some scholars wish to limit what we may take from the Gospels and classify as parables or extended comparisons. Obviously this book interprets 'parables' in the broad sense of stories Jesus told about the kingdom of God. These parables vary strikingly in length – from the one verse of the treasure in the field to the twenty-two verses of the prodigal son. The stories run all the way from mini- or micro-parables to macro-parables.

I might have made other scholars nervous by not relentlessly introducing distinctions between three stages in the formation of the stories which we have: the stage of Jesus' own preaching, that of the transmission of his words in the early communities, and the final stage when the Gospel writers composed the final texts. Beyond question, the language of Jesus underwent modifications as it was passed down and then written up. In what I have presented I have tried to respect the developments which led to the form of the Gospel parables as we have them from Matthew, Mark and Luke. At the same time, I am convinced by the arguments which conclude that the parable material I have used goes back substantially, but not necessarily word for word, to Jesus himself.

As I bring this book to an end, my main worry is that too much commentary could suggest to the ordinary reader that Jesus might not have been the Great Communicator. Where comments proliferate around every word, this might be taken to imply that we need to explain all the moves Jesus made. I shrink from conveying any such implication.

Some wonderful words in the Book of Acts almost picture our present life as being in the womb of the God 'in whom we live and move and have our being' (Acts 17:28). This language catches perfectly the existence of the unborn child, who does not yet look on its mother's face but depends utterly on her for life and being. In the light of those exquisite words, we might well interpret the parables as Jesus' attempt to explain to us babies in the womb what God and God's world are and will be really like. Drawing his stories from our womb-like existence in this world and on this earth, Jesus reveals and initiates our life to come in the new heaven and on the new earth. Through his transforming eye and powerful words, the most ordinary experiences become engrossing vehicles for divine revelation and salvation.

FURTHER READING AND ACKNOWLEDGEMENTS

About the parables in general, readers could profit from Ruth Etchells, *A Reading of the Parables* (London: Darton, Longman & Todd, 1998). On the parable of the prodigal son, Henri Nouwen has left his readers *The Return of the Prodigal Son* (New York/London: Doubleday/Darton, Longman & Todd, 1992).

This book uses the New Revised Standard Version of the Bible, but very occasionally modifies – perhaps I should say corrects – that translation. Living in Italy has made me more conscious than ever that no translation does justice to the original. As the Italians put it, 'the translator is a traitor (*traduttore traditore*)'.

I wish to thank very warmly Michael Heher (who has shown me so much about the work of Flannery O'Connor), Andrew Cusack and Laurence Freeman (who have given me wonderful audiences for some presentations on the parables), and Rocco and Barbara Martino who brought me to share my thoughts on the parables over one memorable weekend with many members of the Order of Malta. My special thanks go also to James Catford, a most intelligent and encouraging editor.

Index of Names